Britain
1900–51

RICHARD RADWAY

Contents

Hodder & Stoughton

A MEMBER OF THE HODDER HEADLINE GROUP

Life in Britain in 1900

What was it like to live in Britain in 1900?

In 1900 most people believed that Great Britain was the most powerful country in the world. Although Britain was a small island it ruled an **empire** which stretched around the globe. One quarter of all the people in the world were ruled by Britain. It was still one of the leading industrial countries in the world. What was it like to live in this country?

A Traffic near the Bank of England in London. At the end of the nineteenth century the horse still dominated the roads, even in the world's largest city.

In 1750 Britain had been a mainly rural country with a population of less than ten million. Most people had lived in villages and many of them had worked on the land. This had all changed by 1900. The population had increased to about 42 million and only about nine per cent of workers had jobs in agriculture. Most people lived in towns. In 1801 there had only been 16 towns with a population of more than 20 000. By 1901 there were almost 160.

Transport was changing as well. In 1900 horse-drawn vehicles were still the main form of transport. There were very few cars in Britain. Until 1896 any car had to be accompanied by a man walking in front carrying a red flag.

> A footman's wages varied depending on the man's height. A six-foot tall footman might be paid 80 pence a week while one who was six inches shorter might only be paid 40 pence. A taller footman was more impressive!

B Trams at the Elephant and Castle in London. Just twenty years later and not a horse to be seen.

There was little point in owning a car if it could only go as fast as a man could walk. However, in public transport the horse did face competition. By 1905 most towns and cities had introduced electric powered trams. These ran on rails and, as source B shows, they didn't exactly make things easy for other road users.

Rich and poor

In 1900 almost no houses had electricity. This meant that there were no vacuum cleaners, washing machines or any of the domestic appliances that we take for granted today. However, this did not matter if you were rich. You were able to employ servants to do all the domestic work.

C A rich English family relaxing.

About three per cent of the population could be described as being very rich. These were the people who earned at least £700 a year. They included the great landowners, wealthy industrialists and the most successful professional men, such as senior judges and senior officers in the armed forces.

> Tea was everyone's standard drink, but it cost eight pence a pound (450 g). Bread was the basic food, with a loaf costing two pence.

The famous cookery writer, Mrs Beeton, suggested that any family with an income of £1000 a year should be able to employ a cook, two maids and a manservant. Servants' wages were low. A maid might be paid only 25 pence a week. So the very rich would be able to employ many more servants. This would leave plenty of time for relaxing.

Below the rich came the middle classes. They might earn between £150 and £700 a year. This would still mean that most of them could employ at least one servant. These people were the shop-keepers and professional people such as lawyers.

The working class made up the rest of the population. The average wage for men who worked in industry was only £1.50 a week and women earned much less. Most of this would go on rent and food. In a survey of York the businessman Rowntree reckoned that a family with three children needed just over one pound a week to cope. He discovered that 40 per cent of the working class in York earned less than this. But even an income of one pound left families with no money for medical expenses, or for any luxuries such as alcohol or gambling. Since people did fall ill, drink and gamble, many more than 40 per cent of families were living in poverty. Life might have been extremely comfortable for the rich in 1900, but it was very tough for the majority of the population.

D A slum in Kensington, London. The very poorest people lived in terrible conditions.

Education

On the other hand, by 1900 every child did go to school. In 1899 the school leaving age was raised to 12. This meant that every child received a basic education at an elementary school. However, only about one child in 80 went on to secondary school. Secondary education was not free and so most working-class people couldn't afford it. Of course the very rich sent their sons to public schools, which aimed to turn out perfect Christian English gentlemen, and most middle-class families did send their children to secondary school. But, in Germany, far more children attended secondary school. As far as education was concerned, Britain was losing out to its new rival.

Q

1 Why do you think that some people felt it was bad for Britain's economic future that so few children went to secondary school?
2 Rowntree estimated that a family needed to earn one pound a week. A maid earned just 25 pence. What does this tell you about the sort of people who became maids? For instance, could you live on your own if you were a maid?

The Changing Political Scene

How were Labour able to replace the Liberals as Britain's second major political party?

Parliament

Britain in 1900 was a parliamentary democracy, just like it is today. This means that a parliament, elected by the people, makes all the laws. Even the Queen could not reject a decision made by parliament. However, in many respects things were very different. The Prime Minister in 1900 was Lord Salisbury. As his name suggests he was a member of the House of Lords. He had not been elected by the people. Indeed the unelected House of Lords was able to block decisions made by the elected House of Commons. Today the House of Lords can only delay measures and the Prime Minister cannot be a member of the Lords. In 1963 Lord Hume had to give up being a lord in order to become the Prime Minister.

Who could vote in 1900?

Today everyone over the age of 18 can vote. This was not the situation in 1900, although things had changed dramatically in the previous 100 years. In 1800 very few people could vote. The system was very unfair, and did not reflect the change in the country which the **Industrial Revolution** had produced. A major city such as Manchester didn't

have any MPs while Gatton in Surrey elected an MP despite having only six houses and one voter. However, the parliamentary Acts of 1832, 1867 and 1884 did greatly increase the number of men who could vote. By 1900 all male householders could vote and no town with fewer than 15 000 voters could elect an MP. This meant that over five million men could vote, just under one third of the adult population. However, no women could vote until 1918. The story of their campaign is told in Chapter 5.

A The percentage of adults who could vote.	
1832	7%
1867	16%
1884	29%

The MPs themselves were generally rich people. They needed to be since an MP was not paid.

The political parties in 1900

The British voting system is of a type known as 'first past the post'. This means that the country is divided into constituencies and the candidate who wins the most votes in a constituency is elected. This tends to produce a two-party system. Those people who are content with the government will vote for the party which is in power. Those people who are not happy with the government will vote for the party which is likely to win enough seats to replace them. Therefore third parties, which the

Parliament ruled the country. It passed all laws on behalf of the people. This was parliamentary democracy in 1900.

B Parliament in 1900.

The House of Lords was made up of hereditary lords. This meant that when a lord died he was replaced by his eldest son. If there wasn't a son then the closest living male relative took over. No one was elected to the Lords.

The House of Commons was made up of MPs elected by the people. But only 29 per cent of the people were allowed to vote.

voters believe are not likely to win enough seats to form a government, tend to win few votes.

The two main parties in Britain in 1900 were the Liberals and the Conservatives. They had dominated politics for much of the nineteenth century and expected to dominate in the twentieth century as well. However, this was not what actually happened. In the first quarter of the century the Labour Party replaced the Liberals as the second major party. The Liberals were to remain a minor party for the rest of the period.

The Conservative Party

In 1900 the Conservatives won the general election with a huge majority. The Boer War, in which Boers in South Africa were trying to break away from the British Empire, was a big factor in this victory. People in Britain voted for the party whose policy was to preserve the empire.

The Conservative Party was traditionally supported by wealthy businessmen and landowners. They believed that the government should let the rich get on with the job of making Britain rich. The government should not interfere with the economy. This was known as *laissez faire*. It meant **free trade**, that is, no duties on imported or exported goods. However, British industries were finding it increasingly difficult to compete with Germany and America and so some people wanted to introduce import duties to make foreign goods more expensive in Britain. This would protect British industries from foreign competition at home, yet it would hurt Britain's exports, as other countries would retaliate by putting up their duties. One group of Conservative MPs, led by Joseph Chamberlain, wanted to increase import duties on German and American goods in order to protect trade within the empire. But the issue divided the party and led to the Conservatives being defeated in the 1906 election.

Despite this defeat, the Conservatives went on to become the most successful party in the first half of the twentieth century. They were in government for much of the time. However, this did not mean that they formed the government. Today we are used to majority governments which rule the country on their own. But various problems in the first half of the twentieth century led to a number of **coalition** governments. This meant that although the Conservatives were usually the largest party in the government, they did not always provide the Prime Minister. For instance, Ramsay MacDonald was the Labour Prime Minister of what was a largely Conservative government from 1931 until 1936.

C The Conservative MP, Joseph Chamberlain, speaking in May 1903.

While we should seek as our chief aim free trade … we will nevertheless … retaliate [fight back] whenever our own interest or our relations between ourselves and our colonies [empire] are threatened by other people.

1905	Conservative
	Liberal
1915	
	Coalition of Conservatives, Liberals and Labour with Liberal Lloyd George as Prime Minister
1918	
	Coalition of Conservatives and a few Liberals with Lloyd George as Prime Minister
1922	
	Conservative
1924	Labour
	Conservative
1929	
1931	Labour
	National (Coalition) Government of Conservatives, Liberals and a few Labour MPs, with Labour Ramsay MacDonald as Prime Minister
1935	
	National Government with Conservative Baldwin as Prime Minister
1937	
	National Government with Conservative Neville Chamberlain as Prime Minister
1940	
	National Government with Conservative Winston Churchill as Prime Minister

D The governments of the period 1900–45. (The Conservatives formed the largest part of all the Coalition Governments of the period.)

Q

1 Look at source C. Why does Chamberlain suggest that import duties on foreign goods should be introduced?
2 What other reason for introducing import duties had been suggested by other people?
3 Why could it be argued that import duties were not in Britain's interest?

THE RISE OF THE LABOUR PARTY

The Liberal and Conservative parties both represented the interests of the rich and the middle classes. There was no party to represent the working class. This was hardly surprising. For most of the nineteenth century the working class did not have the right to vote. The voting acts of 1867 and 1884 finally gave many working men the vote, but the problems which really mattered to working class people – poverty and dangerous working conditions in industry – were not important to most Liberals and Conservatives.

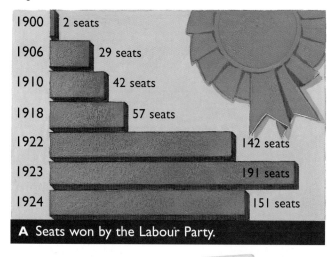

1900	2 seats
1906	29 seats
1910	42 seats
1918	57 seats
1922	142 seats
1923	191 seats
1924	151 seats

A Seats won by the Labour Party.

VOTE FOR

"FROM INDUSTRIAL SLAVERY TO SOCIAL FREEDOM"

HARDIE

B 'Vote for Hardie.' This poster was used by Keir Hardie when he stood for election in Bradford in 1896.

As a result of the lack of action by the government on these issues, socialist societies became increasingly popular. Then, in 1893, James Keir Hardie founded the Independent Labour Party (ILP). Its main aim was to get socialists elected to parliament. This meant that it was a democratic socialist party, unlike the Communists in Russia who believed that **socialism** could only be achieved through a **revolution**.

In 1900 the Labour Representative Committee (LRC) was formed. This was an alliance of the trade unions and a number of the socialist societies, including the ILP. At this stage the LRC did not look like it was going to be a success. In the election of October 1900 only two LRC MPs were elected. One of these was Keir Hardie himself. Very few trade unions were involved. Only 40 agreed to back the LRC, even though there were over 1000 active trade unions in Britain in 1900. The really large unions, such as the miners and the textile workers, did not join.

However, over the next three years membership of the LRC trebled. The main reason for this was a court decision in 1901 known as the Taff Vale Judgement. In 1900 railway workers on the Taff Vale Railway in South Wales went on strike. During the strike the company lost money as no trains were running. The company sued the rail workers' union for the money they had lost and the court declared that the union would have to pay up. Before Taff Vale most union members and leaders supported going on strike to improve working conditions. After Taff Vale it appeared that unions could no longer afford to go on strike, so getting MPs elected to parliament became a much more popular option as a way of improving the conditions for workers. In 1906 the LRC became known as the Labour Party.

The problem of the third party

In the early years of the twentieth century the Labour Party was very much the third party. As mentioned earlier, the British 'first past the post' system makes it very difficult for third parties to win many seats. In 1906 the Labour Party attempted to overcome this problem by making a deal with the Liberal Party. They agreed not to put up candidates against each other in certain constituencies. The result was that 29 Labour candidates were elected.

However, working people had another problem. Most MPs were rich. They needed to be, since MPs were not paid. Labour MPs could survive only because they were backed by trade unions, who paid them a wage. But in 1909 a court judgement, known as the Osborn judgement, declared that this was illegal. It looked as though the Labour Party would collapse. It was saved by the Liberal government, which in 1911 introduced a salary of £400 for every MP. Then in 1913 it passed the Trade Union Act, which allowed trade unions to give money to political parties.

After the war the 1918 Representation of the People Act gave the vote to all men over 21 and all women over 30 who were house owners. Veterans of the war were allowed to vote at 19. This increased the number of voters from seven million to 21 million. The new leader of the Labour Party, James Ramsay MacDonald, was determined to make people think of his party as the official opposition party. This would mean that they would vote for Labour when they were fed up with the government. Sources A and D show just how successful he was. In January 1924 he became the first ever Labour Prime Minister. The reasons for his success are explored on page 8.

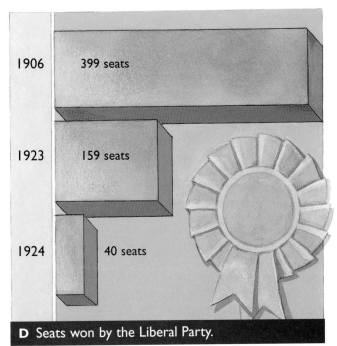

1906	399 seats
1923	159 seats
1924	40 seats

D Seats won by the Liberal Party.

FORCED FELLOWSHIP.

Suspicious-looking Party. "ANY OBJECTION TO MY COMPANY, GUV'NOR? I'M AGOIN' YOUR WAY"—(aside) "AND FURTHER."

C A cartoon showing an interpretation of the relationship between the Labour and Liberal parties. The figure on the left in the cloth cap represents the Labour Party. The figure on the right in the top hat represents the Liberal Party. Note the club in the hand of the Labour Party.

Q

1 In which year did the Labour Party gain the most MPs?
2 What reasons can you find to explain why the Labour Party did so much better in 1906 than the LRC had done in the election of 1900?
3 Look at source B.
  a) Look at the top left hand corner of the poster. What does this suggest that socialism will bring for working people?
  b) Look at the bottom of the poster. What are the problems for working people?
  c) Do you think that this poster would encourage people to vote for Keir Hardy? Explain your answer.
4 Look at source C.
  a) How does the cartoonist show the Labour Party?
  b) How does the cartoonist show the Liberal Party?
  c) What does the cartoonist suggest about the relationship between the Labour Party and the Liberals?
  d) Do you agree with this view?

THE STRANGE DEATH OF THE LIBERAL PARTY

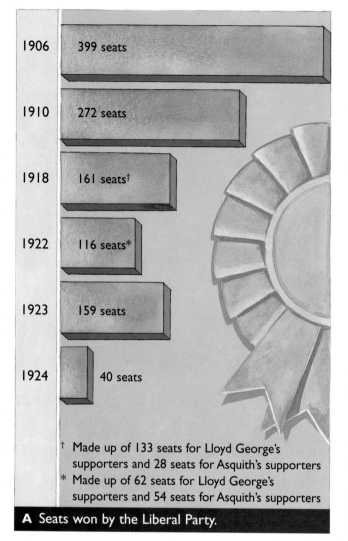

1906	399 seats
1910	272 seats
1918	161 seats†
1922	116 seats*
1923	159 seats
1924	40 seats

† Made up of 133 seats for Lloyd George's supporters and 28 seats for Asquith's supporters
* Made up of 62 seats for Lloyd George's supporters and 54 seats for Asquith's supporters

A Seats won by the Liberal Party.

The Liberal Party was the second great party at the beginning of the twentieth century. In 1906 the Liberal Party won a massive election victory with 399 seats against the Conservative Party's 157. In the election campaign the Liberals promised to introduce social reform to help the mass of ordinary people. They would help the old and the weak. This was a message which the voters wanted to hear. Campbell-Bannerman became the new Prime Minister. Yet, less than 20 years later, in 1924, the Liberals won just 40 seats. Since that time they have remained the third party of British politics. Why did this happen?

Before the First World War both the Labour and the Liberal parties were the parties who supported social reform. However, since the Liberal Party was the only one likely to be able to form a government the Labour Party won few seats. The great reforms of 1906–11 may not have gone far enough for some reformers but they showed that the Liberal Party could carry out its promises. They even succeeded in overcoming the opposition of the House of Lords (see Chapter 3). There seemed to be every reason to believe that the Liberal Party would remain the party of reform in the minds of the British voters.

The Liberals and the First World War

The First World War changed this. At the beginning of the war Britain had a Liberal government led by Asquith. But the war did not lead to the quick victory that had been expected and Asquith was blamed. In 1915 he formed a coalition government with some Conservatives and the Labour leader, Arthur Henderson, along with 12 Liberals. However, many people felt that Asquith was not fully committed to the decisive action that would be required to win the war. He had not been in favour of introducing **conscription**, which means ordering all young men to join up to fight. Along with Lord Kitchener, the War Minister, Asquith preferred people to volunteer. Other members of the government, led by another Liberal, Lloyd George, demanded the introduction of conscription. They felt that Britain would not have enough troops to win the war if only volunteers were used. In fact British losses in 1915 were so great that in January 1916 conscription had to be introduced. Then, in the second half of 1916, the Battle of the Somme produced terrible casualties rather than the hoped-for victory.

The popular newspapers, such as the *Daily Mail* and the *Daily Express*, demanded that Asquith be replaced by Lloyd George. In December 1916 Lloyd George became the new Prime Minister. The Liberal Party was split down the middle. About half of the Liberal MPs supported Lloyd George. However, half of them continued to support Asquith who remained the official party leader. The split continued after the war and so there were now two Liberal Parties. Voters who wanted social reform turned to the Labour Party. Those who could not face socialism turned to the Conservatives. Lloyd George remained Prime Minister, but he was now at the head of what was essentially a Conservative government since it was supported by almost three times as many Conservative MPs as Liberals.

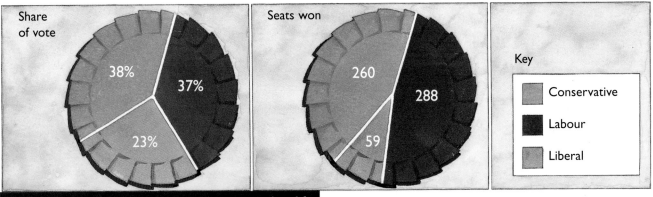

B The British 'first past the post' system makes life very tough for third parties, as shown by the results of the 1929 election.

C Paul Adelman on the causes of the Liberal decline (from 'The Decline of the Liberal Party' in *Britain 1918–51*, edited by P Catterall, 1994).

It has been argued by some writers, notably George Dangerfield in his melodramatic *Strange Death of Liberal England*, that the seeds of Liberal decline were already apparent in the years 1910–14. They argue that the Liberal Party was faced with a combination of problems – opposition of the House of Lords, strikes, Suffragettes, armed opposition in Ireland – which, together, fatally undermined its strength and confidence.

E Adapted from *The Downfall of the Liberal Party 1914–35* (1968). Professor T Wilson considers the importance of the First World War.

The Liberal Party may be compared to an individual who, after a period of good health and great exercise, experienced symptoms of illness (Ireland, strikes, the Suffragettes). Before a thorough diagnosis could be made, he was involved in an accident with a runaway bus (the First World War), which mounted the pavement and ran him over. After lingering painfully, he died. A controversy has continued ever since as to what killed him. One medical school argues that even without the bus he would soon have died … Another school goes further, and says that the encounter with the bus would not have proved fatal had not the victim's health already been seriously weakened. Neither of these views is accepted here … The outbreak of the First World War began a process of break-up in the Liberal Party which by 1918 had reduced it to ruins.

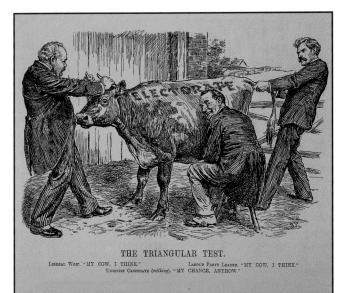

THE TRIANGULAR TEST.

LIBERAL WHIP. "MY COW, I THINK."   LABOUR PARTY LEADER. "MY COW, I THINK."
UNIONIST CANDIDATE (*milking*). "MY CHANCE, ANYHOW."

D The Conservatives get the milk while the Liberals and the Labour Party struggle over the cow. In other words the Conservatives will win the election because the votes of those people who oppose the Conservatives will be divided between Labour and the Liberals. This cartoon comes from *Punch*, 10 July 1912. Look at source B. Who has won the struggle for the cow?

Q

1 Look at sources C and E. In source E Professor Wilson describes two 'medical schools' of opinion about the death of the Liberal Party. The first is that the Liberal Party was so ill from previous difficulties that it would have 'died' even if the First World War had not happened. The second 'school' says that the First World War would not have killed the Liberals if the party had not already been weak. In which of the 'medical schools' described in source E would you place Dangerfield's explanation for the death of the Liberal Party?

2 Which explanation does Professor Wilson believe?

3 What evidence can you find to back up Professor Wilson's interpretation for the decline of the Liberal Party?

3 *The Beginnings of the Welfare State*

To what extent were the lives of working people improved in the early twentieth century?

Poverty and the working class

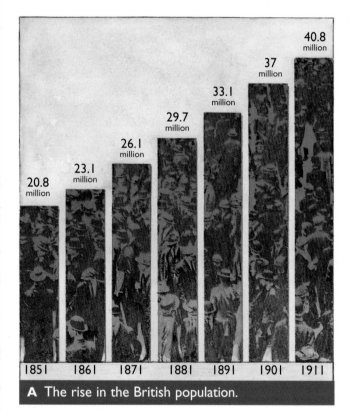

A The rise in the British population.

20.8 million 1851
23.1 million 1861
26.1 million 1871
29.7 million 1881
33.1 million 1891
37 million 1901
40.8 million 1911

B A Manchester slum at the end of the nineteenth century.

C Lloyd George, the Liberal Chancellor of the Exchequer, speaking in 1909.

Help for the aged and the deserving poor – it is time it was done. It is a shame that a rich country like ours – probably the richest in the world – should allow those who have toiled all their days to end in poverty and starvation.

At the beginning of the twentieth century many British people lived in terrible poverty. Part of the reason for this can be seen in source A. The population of Britain had risen dramatically in the second half of the nineteenth century. However, it was not simply the number of people which created the problem. It was where they were living. There were fewer and fewer jobs in the countryside. Therefore people were forced to live in towns in the hope of finding jobs. In 1801 only 25 per cent of the population lived in towns of more than 10 000 people. By 1901 75 per cent of the British people lived in such towns. The result was terrible overcrowding. Many people were forced to live in slum housing. Overcrowding and poor sanitation, such as a lack of toilets, produced disease. By 1913 half a million people a year were still dying from diseases such as pneumonia, bronchitis and tuberculosis.

At the opening of the twentieth century Britain was arguably the richest country in the world. Yet for many of the working class the problem was not just that they lived in terrible conditions. They were often laid off when there was no work and this meant no money coming into the household. Once they were too old to work, there were no pensions for them. They were forced to rely on their family to help them survive.

The governments of the nineteenth century had done very little to help. They did not believe that it was the job of the government to get involved in ordinary people's lives. Nevertheless, in 1875 the Public Health Act was introduced. This made it the duty of local councils to keep sewers clean and to remove rubbish from the streets. This was done in order to try and reduce the spread of disease. In the same year the government also gave councils the power to clear slums and replace them with better houses. However, although councils now had the power, they were not ordered to carry out slum clearance. Most councils did nothing.

Education

It [education] would teach them to despise their role in life, instead of making them good servants in agriculture and other employment. It would enable them to read pamphlets which encouraged them to rebel ... it would lead them to disobey their superiors.

E The report of the Royal Commission on Technical Instruction in 1884.

The one point in which Germany is overwhelmingly superior to England is in schools ... The dense ignorance so common among workmen in England is unknown.

For much of the nineteenth century there was little in the way of schooling provided for working-class children. Some people thought it was wrong to educate working-class children. They believed that educated working-class children would not want to work in factories. They would become dissatisfied with their life and then they would rebel. However, as industries became more complex an educated workforce was needed. In the late nineteenth century the government introduced elementary education, up to the age of 12, for all children. In 1902 it put education under the control of local councils and gave them the power to open secondary schools as well. But secondary schooling was not free.

'New Liberalism'

In 1906 the Liberals won the general election with a huge majority. They gained 399 seats while the Conservatives won only 157. The new Prime Minister was Campbell-Bannerman. The new government was determined to introduce reforms to help working people. The rise of the Labour Party was a sign that working people were not happy with the two big parties. Between 1916 and 1919 the government introduced measures to deal with the problems of unemployment, ill health and old age (see pages 12–13).

The creators of this 'New Liberalism' were Lloyd George and Winston Churchill. Both hoped that this concern for the poor would win votes. But perhaps more important was the fact that Lloyd George had visited Germany, the country which was quickly developing into the new industrial leader of Europe. Germany already had health insurance and old age pensions. It was hoped that the reforms in Britain would produce a stronger and fitter workforce which would be able to meet the challenge of Germany.

Drink made poverty worse. In York, the average working-class family spent about a quarter of their income on alcohol.

F Winston Churchill, writing in 1901.

I have been reading a book by Mr Rowntree called *Poverty* which has impressed me very much ... it is evident from the figures that the American labourer is a stronger, larger, healthier, better fed and consequently more efficient animal than a large proportion of our own population ... I see little glory in an empire which rules the waves, and is unable to flush its sewers.

Q

1 Look at source B. Why did so many people in Britain live in conditions like these at the beginning of the twentieth century?
2 Why had governments done little to help?
3 In the late nineteenth and early twentieth centuries British governments had made education available for poor children. In 1911 the Liberals introduced a National Insurance scheme which gave free medical care for workers. Why was this done?
   a) Look at sources E and F. Find a reason which is common to both sources.
   b) What other reason can you find for the introduction of the Liberal reforms?

THE LIBERAL WELFARE REFORMS

In 1906 the Liberal government introduced the Workmen's Compensation Act. This covered all workers who earned less than £250 a year. If they were badly injured by an accident at work they would still get half of their wages.

In the same year an Act was passed which meant that local councils had to provide school meals for children. The following year another Act introduced medical inspections for all school children.

The problem of the elderly was tackled when old age pensions were introduced in 1908. The Act gave a pension of five shillings (25 pence) a week to single people over 70 and 7s 6d (37½ pence) to married couples. The government then turned its attention to the unemployed and in 1909 introduced the first Labour Exchanges. Their purpose was to help unemployed people to find jobs.

Although medicine improved considerably in the nineteenth century it was not free. **Friendly societies** had been set up to provide health insurance but the poor and the unemployed could not afford to pay the premiums. In 1911 the National Insurance Act was introduced. This had two parts. Part One set up a fund to help pay for medical care for low paid workers. Better paid workers were still expected to pay for their own medical care. Everyone who had a job but earned less than £160 a year had to pay 4d (1½ pence) a week into a fund. Employers had to pay another 3d for each worker and the government added a further 2d. In return workers could go and see a doctor for free. They also received ten shillings (50 pence) a week if they could not go to work because they were too sick. Part Two gave further help to the unemployed. This helped those workers in certain industries, such as building, where men were regularly laid off work. It set up another fund to which workers and employers paid 2½d (one pence) a week. This money would then be used to give seven shillings (35 pence) a week to anyone who was unemployed, though only for the first 15 weeks.

How far did the reforms go?

The Liberal reforms established the foundations of the welfare state. 35 years later the Labour government would build on these foundations (see pages 58–59). But for now the reforms were just a beginning. They were a long way short of solving all the problems. In particular they did not cover all poor people.

Firstly, medical care was only provided for the worker. It did not cover wives and children. Hospital treatment was not included and neither were dental and eye care. Secondly, the old age pensions only covered people of 70 and over. This meant that there were still a lot of old people who got nothing at all. Finally, the unemployment insurance only covered about two million workers. There were millions more who were still not

A Lloyd George speaking to a crowd in Wales in 1909. He declared that 'It is essential that we should make every necessary provision for the defence of our country. But surely it is equally important that we should make it a country even better worth defending.'

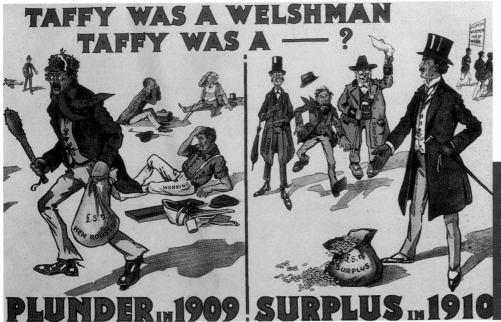

TAFFY WAS A WELSHMAN
TAFFY WAS A —— ?

PLUNDER IN 1909 ! SURPLUS IN 1910

B A Conservative Party poster. It shows Lloyd George first as a mugger and then giving the money away. The figures who have been mugged by Lloyd George are the trader, the house builder and the working man.

covered. Also the benefits were only to last for a short period of time. The amounts paid were very small. They were not meant to be enough to live on, just enough to keep people going during an emergency.

Mr Balfour's poodles

The Liberal reforms might not have helped everyone who needed help, but they were still going to cost a lot of money. At the same time Britain was engaged in an arms race with Germany. New battleships, known as Dreadnoughts, needed to be built. The reforms and the ships would together cost £15 million. Taxes would have to be increased. In 1909 the new Chancellor of the Exchequer, Lloyd George, presented what he called his 'People's Budget'. Income tax for ordinary people would not be increased. However, those who earned more than £3000 a year would pay just under one per cent more.

Those who earned over £5000 a year would pay an extra super tax of 2.5 per cent. On top of this death duties would be increased, along with land taxes. The rich would pay for the reforms.

The House of Commons passed the budget but the mainly Conservative House of Lords rejected it. Without the support of the House of Lords these changes would not be legal. Lloyd George described the Lords as 'Mr Balfour's poodles' (Balfour was the leader of the Conservatives). He also described the Lords as '500 ordinary men, chosen accidentally from the ranks of the unemployed'. The Lords did not back down until the following year, when the King threatened to create enough Liberal lords to pass the budget. The House of Lords was forced to agree that never again would it be able to defeat a budget.

C An extract from the novel *Lark Rise to Candleford* by Flora Thompson (1939). She had once been a post office worker who handed out old age pensions.

When the Old Age Pensions began, life was transformed for such aged cottagers [old people]. They were relieved of anxiety. They were suddenly rich. Independent for life! At first when they went down to the Post Office to draw it [their pension] tears of gratitude would run down the cheeks of some, and they would say as they picked up their money, 'God Bless that Lord George'.

Q

1 What did Lloyd George mean when he described the House of Lords as 'Mr Balfour's poodles'?
2 Look at source B. What impression does it give of the 1909 budget? Did the figures lying on the floor really suffer from the budget?
3 What impression of the reforms is given in source C?
4 Source C is a novel. Do you think it gives an accurate picture? (Think about the **provenance** of the source. Who wrote it? Was the writer in a position to comment?)

4

The Impact of The First World War

Why did so many men volunteer to fight in the First World War?

At midnight on 4 August 1914 Britain declared war on Germany. When the war began Britain had an army of only 100 000 men. This was immediately sent to France as the British Expeditionary Force (BEF). But as the two sides dug in along the Western Front vast numbers of soldiers were required to fight the **war of attrition**. At first the British relied on volunteers. Posters were used to encourage people to join up. Lord Kitchener became the new Minister of War and he asked for 100 000 men to enlist. They did so in huge numbers. By the end of the first week 175 000 had volunteered and by the end of the first month this figure had increased to 750 000. In total two and a half million men volunteered to fight.

A A government recruiting poster.

YOUR COUNTRY'S CALL

Isn't this worth fighting for?
ENLIST NOW

B Kitchener's face stares out from this recruitment poster.

'YOU ARE THE MAN I WANT'

C An extract from 'The Volunteer' by Herbert Asquith, who was the son of the Prime Minister and who served in the war.

Here lies a clerk who half his life had spent
Toiling at ledgers in a city grey,
Thinking that so his days would drift away
With no lance broken in life's tournament.
Yet ever 'twixt the books and his bright eyes
The gleaming eagles of the legions came,
And horsemen, charging under phantom skies,
Went thundering past beneath the oriflamme
[The oriflamme is a sacred flag of France]

Why did so many men join up?

Many people joined up out of patriotism, because their king and country had asked them. Kitchener was the popular face of the country and his finger pointed from countless posters. People believed that it was Britain's moral duty to defend Belgium from the German bullies. As Rupert Brooke wrote: 'Now God be thanked who has matched us with His hour'. God and Britain were on the same side.

People were encouraged to believe that the war would soon be over. The popular view was that it would be 'over by Christmas'.

"A Happy New Year to our Gallant Soldiers!"

VICTORY 1915

You can make it certain if you
JOIN NOW

D Victory 1915. A government recruiting poster. There is no mention of the stalemate on the Western Front.

There would be a quick, glorious victory followed by a hero's return. Few people imagined the horrors ahead. Besides, for many young men life contained little adventure. They had left school and gone to work in their local town. Few could afford holidays. The war provided an opportunity to break out of this dull life. The posters promised a world of adventure and excitement. When the war was over they would be treated as heroes.

Another reason for joining up was that many of the working class in Britain were very poor. Large numbers worked in industries which regularly laid them off without pay when there was little work. The army offered them a regular wage and regular meals.

Posters were used to make those who had not joined up feel guilty. In particular women were encouraged to convince their husbands and boyfriends to join up. This took its most extreme form in the white feather campaign. Women would present men who had not joined up with a white feather, to suggest that they were cowards.

Others were persuaded to enlist by the idea of Pals' Battalions. Friends from a local area were encouraged to join up together. Sometimes people who worked together joined together. Sometimes it was men who played together in a local team. As friends trained and fought together they would help to keep each other's spirits up, and give each other courage. But the problem with this became clear once these Pals' Battalions became involved in heavy fighting. Then whole groups of men from the same town or village died together. The effect on the local community could be devastating.

E The London Cyclists. Pals' Battalions such as this one offered friends and adventure.

How effective was Kitchener's volunteer army?

The volunteer army was certainly a tremendous achievement. It was the largest volunteer army ever raised by any country. In fact, it was so big that the government had not been prepared for so many men so quickly. There were few uniforms and few weapons. Volunteers spent the winter of 1914 living in tents and training with sticks instead of guns. Perhaps more importantly there were few people to train them. Kitchener decided to send all of the regular army to fight in France. This meant that the volunteers were mainly trained by old soldiers who came out of retirement to help. These men had last fought when Victoria was still Queen. They had little idea of current tactics and the effectiveness of new weapons.

F Rifleman Bernard Britland was one of those who volunteered in September 1914. In January 1915 he wrote this letter to his family.

The Sergeant-Major was so [impressed] with the progress we made that he served 25 rifles out to the smartest of us. I was one of the 25 so you can bet I didn't half feel proud of myself. The draft that was here before us were two or three weeks before they got their rifles and we had them in three days so that is something to be proud of isn't it?

We are being well fed here. This morning we had a tin of sardines each for breakfast … For dinner we generally have potatoes, haricot beans, roast meat, stewed meat, cabbage and green peas so there is plenty of variety.

G A British soldier describes how he felt after volunteering.

I went home each evening with my rifle on my shoulder … Girls smiled at me, men looked at me with respect, the bus drivers wished me luck and refused to take my money for my fare.

Q

1 Read source F. What is Rifleman Britland most proud of?
2 What reasons for joining up can you find in sources F and G?
3 Why do you think that young men might be impressed by posters D and E?
4 Using all seven sources on this page, explain why so many men volunteered in 1914.

THE GOVERNMENT IN THE FIRST WORLD WAR

Key Issue **To what extent did the role of government change during the First World War?**

In the nineteenth century the Liberals and the Conservatives had generally agreed that the government should not get involved with the day-to-day life of ordinary people. Safety rules had been imposed in factories but in general most people were not affected by the workings of the government. However, at the beginning of the twentieth century the Liberal reforms had begun to create a welfare state. Government was becoming more involved. This trend was accelerated by the First World War. Suddenly the government was forced to take charge of large parts of daily life. Five million men were ordered into the army, the publication of news was controlled, even the time on the clock was changed.

Taking control of industry

During the war the government took control of those industries which were most important to winning the war such as steel production, shipbuilding, mining and the railways. This ensured that raw materials, food and vital supplies got to where they were needed, and that factories had enough power.

In 1915 Lloyd George became the first ever Minister of Munitions. Earlier that year there had been a scandal because the generals claimed that the British army did not have enough artillery shells to compete with the Germans. Lloyd George was determined to increase munitions production. He used his powers to introduce what was known as **dilution**. This meant that semi-skilled and unskilled workers were allowed to do work which had previously only been carried out by skilled workers.

The main effect of Lloyd George's changes was that almost one million women were employed in the munitions industry by 1918. Also 20 000 new munitions factories had been set up. By 1918 Britain was actually managing to produce enough weapons and ammunition for its army of four million men. Lloyd George also ordered far more machine-guns than the generals requested. He realised that they were the key weapon in trench warfare. Britain began the war with just 1330 machine-guns but ended it with 240 000. Lloyd George was so successful that in December 1916 he became Prime Minister.

Possibly the most successful trench weapon was the Stokes mortar. Kitchener and the War Office rejected it when it was offered to them. Lloyd George managed to get an Indian Maharajah to pay for its production.

The limit on pub opening hours was finally abolished in 1989. It was only meant to last until the end of the First World War!

DORA – the Defence of the Realm Acts

The Defence of the Realm Acts (DORA) were a series of measures designed to give the government control over many aspects of life. The first of them was passed in 1914. One of the Acts cut down the length of time that pubs could open. Before the war pubs were allowed to open from early morning and so workers sometimes arrived at work already drunk. Drunkenness meant that workers didn't work so hard, and it could be a real danger in the munitions industry. Beer was also watered down to make it less alcoholic and the price of beer was raised to make it too expensive to get drunk.

'British summer time' was also introduced. The government ordered that clocks should be put forward. This was done to create an extra hour of daylight so that workers, particularly on farms, could work for longer.

Newspapers were **censored** so that their reports of battles did not give vital information to the Germans. Soldiers' letters home to their families were also censored.

> **A** A letter to the *Daily Mirror*, May 1916.
>
> **The government may pass fifty Daylight Saving Bills but I for one shall not alter my watches and clocks to play childish games of 'let's pretend'.**

Conscription

By 1916 the number of men volunteering was far less than in the early stages of the war. It was now obvious that there would be no quick victory. The large lists of casualties being published in newspapers meant that people began to realise that this war did not lead to glory. Therefore, for the first time ever, a British government introduced conscription. Men were ordered to fight in the war. The Military Service Act of January 1916 called up all unmarried men between the ages of 18 and 41. In May this was extended to cover all married men as well. Only workers in essential industries could avoid conscription. This meant miners, train drivers and munitions workers.

Tax

Fighting a war on such a scale was extremely expensive. The government increased income tax by 500 per cent. How times had changed. In 1909 the House of Lords had been upset that the rich were to pay just 2.5 per cent more in tax. Free trade was also sacrificed as import duties were introduced on luxury goods such as cars and clocks.

Strikes

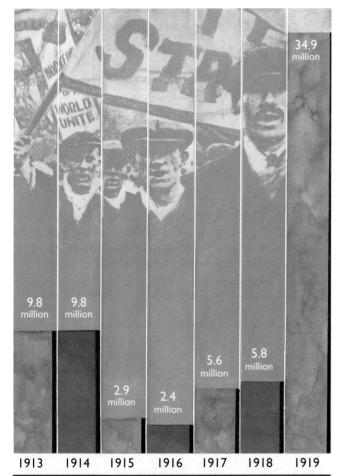

B Working days lost through strikes. This means that the number of workers on strike is multiplied by the number of days on strike. Therefore nine million working days could mean nine million workers on strike for one day or it could mean one million workers on strike for nine days.

9.8 million	9.8 million	2.9 million	2.4 million	5.6 million	5.8 million	34.9 million
1913	1914	1915	1916	1917	1918	1919

C 'A striking contrast.' This cartoon comes from the Christmas 1918 edition of *The Dump* – a newspaper produced once a year by troops in France.

Many skilled workers were unhappy that their unions had accepted dilution. They were also unhappy that many companies were making large profits from supplying the war effort. The workers often felt that the official trade union leaders were not defending the rights of workers. Therefore they elected fellow workers to represent them. These men were known as shop stewards. They were often much more willing to call strikes than the official leaders. However, in 1915 the government made it illegal for anyone in the munitions industry to go on strike against dilution.

Q

1 Why was the government so concerned about the munitions industry?
2 Give an example of another industry which was vital to the war effort and explain why this was so.
3 a) Who produced source C?
   b) What is the cartoonist's opinion of the workers back in Britain?
4 Look at source B. Does it back up the cartoonist?
5 'The British people enthusiastically supported government measures to win the war.' Using your own knowledge and the sources on pages 14–17, explain whether you agree with this interpretation.

LIFE ON THE HOME FRONT

In past European wars people in Britain had been protected from the day-to-day effects. Cities in Europe might be burnt to the ground and people might die of starvation as crops were destroyed, but the British people were safe on their island. The First World War would be different. For the first time civilians would find that the war could be brought to their own front door. Food became increasingly scarce as the war went on. Also, for the first time ever British people were attacked by bombs falling from the sky.

Food

A Mrs Archie Graham reports on the situation in Newton Abbot in Devon in 1918.

No-one has had any cheese for a long time; butter is very hard to get and even margarine is not to be had. A small grocer's shop was 'rushed' a few day's ago: I found a huge crowd when I passed – the women and children were packed in a tight mass right out into the road. I made them let me pass through on the path, and I asked a woman what was going on. 'Oh, margarine,' she said.

Before the war Britain had imported large amounts of food. Bread was the basic food for a large percentage of the population but most of the wheat came from distant countries like Canada. In 1915 the Germans decided to try and starve the British into submission by attacking merchant shipping bringing supplies into the country. Their weapon was the submarine, the U-boat. In 1915 the Germans had only 21 U-boats but as they built more they became very successful. By the end of the war they had sunk 11 million tons of merchant shipping. In April 1917 Britain had just six weeks of grain left, and starvation threatened.

Food shortages created a real problem for the government. Prices shot up. If people could not afford to buy food they were likely to strike for higher wages. In 1915 the Board of Education allowed children to miss school to work on farms. In 1917 the government decided to control the price of grain for bread. A similar arrangement was introduced for potatoes. In effect a maximum price was introduced for both bread and potatoes. The government gave money to farmers so that they did not make a loss at these prices. People were encouraged to eat less bread. In 1916 the

King issued a proclamation asking people to eat 25 per cent less bread and not to use flour in their other cooking.

B A government poster to encourage people to eat less bread. Wheat imports had to get past the German U-boats.

In 1917 the Women's Land Army was also set up. Its purpose was to encourage women to work on farms and replace the men who had gone to fight in the war. However, it was heavy work and was never as popular as other jobs for women. Only 48 000 women joined the Land Army, although there were 260 000 places to be filled.

C War allotments in a London suburb. An official painting by Dorothy Coke. People were also encouraged to dig up their lawns and grow their own potatoes to make sure there was enough food.

In 1918 the government was forced to introduce food rationing. In February rationing was introduced in London and the south east. In July it was extended to the rest of the country. Britain really was the 'home front', for rationing meant that everyone was making a sacrifice. Basic foods like meat, bread, sugar, butter and margarine could only be bought with a ration card in fixed amounts. The amount of food you could buy depended on your job. People in manual work got more food than those in office jobs. Teenage boys got more than girls.

Bombs from the sky

IT IS FAR BETTER TO FACE THE BULLETS THAN TO BE KILLED AT HOME BY A BOMB

JOIN THE ARMY AT ONCE & HELP TO STOP AN AIR RAID

GOD SAVE THE KING

D A recruitment poster showing a Zeppelin flying over St Paul's Cathedral in London.

Another major change for the British people was that they were brought into the front line of the war. On 19 January 1915 the first Zeppelin raid took place. Zeppelins were giant airships which were filled with hydrogen. They could fly higher than the aircraft of the time and so seemed invulnerable as they silently glided across English skies. In 1915 there were 20 Zeppelin raids which killed 188 people. During the entire war bombs dropped by Zeppelins caused 564 deaths. However, on 3 September 1916 Lieutenant Leefe Robinson managed to get his plane up to a Zeppelin and shot it down. He was immediately awarded the Victoria Cross. After that other fighter planes were able to repeat his attack and the Zeppelins became less of a threat.

In 1917 the Germans started to use a new tactic. The long distance bomber aeroplane was introduced. This could carry a much heavier bomb than the Zeppelin. On 13 June 1917 162 people were killed and a further 432 were injured in a single raid on London. The government reacted by introducing a blackout throughout the country. There were no street lights at night. Factories were ordered to stop work if Zeppelins or bombers were spotted nearby.

E Mr Ernest Cooper, the Town Clerk of Southwold in Suffolk, describes the shooting down of a Zeppelin in his diary, 25 January 1917.

At 3.30 [at night] there was a big burst of flame in the sky over Southwold House and we saw it was a Zeppelin alight. She soon broke in two and then began to descend in a wavy line, roaring flames at the head and a long tail of sparks and smoke far up behind. She came down very slowly at first and I had a good view with my glasses [binoculars] … It was a great sight and the people who were out all cheered and those who were in bed came running out in their night dresses … The Capt. of the Zepp and two men landed alive which seems almost incredible but we hear one died afterwards. I think 17 were killed.

Q

1 Look at sources B and C. How do they help you to understand how the British dealt with the problem of food shortages?
2 Read source A. How does it help to explain why the government introduced rationing in 1918?
3 What other reasons can you think of to explain why the government introduced rationing?
4 What evidence can you find that the British people were frightened by the Zeppelin attacks? Was this fear justified?
5 In what ways did the British government increase its powers as a result of U-boats and Zeppelin attacks?

ATTITUDES TO THE WAR

The alien threat

A An attack on a German owned shop in London in 1915.

B An American recruitment poster. It was not only the British government which stirred up hatred against the Germans.

C Sybil Morrison remembers the reaction when the first Zeppelin was shot down on 3 September 1916.

It was like a big cigar I suppose and all of the bag part had caught fire … it was roaring with flames; blue, red, purple. And it seemed to come down slowly instead of falling down with a bang. And we knew that there were about 60 people in it … and that they were roasting to death. Of course you weren't supposed to feel any pity for your enemies, nevertheless I was appalled to see the kind, good-hearted British people dancing about in the streets at the sight of 60 people being burnt alive – clapping and singing and cheering. And my own friends – delighted. When I said I was appalled that anyone could be pleased to see such a terrible sight they said 'But they're Germans, they're the enemy' – not human beings.

At the start of the war the Aliens Restriction Act was passed. This placed very great restrictions on anyone who lived in Britain but had not been born there. As a result over 32 000 people were interned, which means imprisoned without trial. Their only crime was not to be born in Britain. It was felt that they could not be trusted. Over 28 000 aliens were also deported – sent back to their native country. These actions were backed up by government **propaganda**. People wanted to believe this propaganda. There were attacks on shops which were owned by people with German names. It was widely believed that German soldiers in Belgium were killing babies with their bayonets. Fifty years after the war my own great-uncle, who was gassed at Ypres, could still insist to my mother that the only good German was a dead one!

This hatred of Germans soon became a hatred of anyone thought to be foreign. In 1917 there were attacks on Jews in Leeds and London.

D Report of the Chief Constable of Leeds, 4 June 1917.

[In Bridge Street] every Jewish shop widow was smashed and the street was littered with fragments of glass and the remnants of goods … in no case was a shop occupied by a British subject molested.

The 'men who march away'

When the war broke out there was cheering. Men volunteered in huge numbers. They would march to war confident of victory. The bullies must be defeated. When the 18-year-old Bert Chaney left his house to go to war on 4 August 1914 his mother kissed him goodbye and said, 'Be a good boy. Have a good time.' Men couldn't get to the war quickly enough. It might soon be over and their chance of glory gone forever.

E An extract from a poem written by Thomas Hardy, who was 74 when the war broke out.

In our heart of hearts believing
Victory crowns the just,
And that braggarts [bullies] must
Surely bite the dust,
Press we to the field ungrieving,
In our heart of hearts believing
Victory crowns the just.

Hence the faith and fire within us
Men who march away.

Yet as the war dragged on people's attitudes began to change. Ever longer lists of the dead began to appear in newspapers. Families all over the country received dreaded telegrams telling them of the death of a husband, father, son or brother. In 1990, shortly before she died, May Brandon remembered that the only time she ever saw her father cry was when he received the telegram which told of the death of her brother, George, just two days before the end of the war.

The bells began to ring

Finally, at the eleventh hour of the eleventh day of the eleventh month, an armistice came into effect. It had been signed six hours earlier. The war was over. Britain and the Empire had lost almost one million men. Germany had lost two million. Not surprisingly it would be known as the Great War.

F Celebrations in London, November 1918. These celebrations continued for three days and in the end the police had to be sent in to break them up.

G An extract from the diary of Ernest Cooper, 11 November 1918.

Flags soon came out, and the bells began to ring and a few of us adjourned to the Mayor's house and cracked some bottles of Fizz. An impromptu meeting was called and the Mayor read the official telegram from the Swan Balcony. Some soldiers came up on a wagon with the kaiser in effigy [a model of the German King], which they tied to the Town Pump and burnt amidst cheers.

H The reaction of Rifleman Harold Clegg, who was in hospital in England on 11 November.

We were all sitting at our mid-day meal on November 11th, when the matron entered with a telegram in her hand … It was a complete surprise to us to hear that the armistice had been signed. Somehow the news did not convey much to us; the fact that the war was ended was news that had come too late; it mattered little to most of those seated in the dining hall at Elswick whether the war finished or whether it continued for years … Had the news come two years earlier it might have been of interest to us.

Q

1 Read source C. How did most people seem to react to the Germans that day?
2 What reasons can you think of to explain this?
3 Read source H. How can you explain the reaction of Rifleman Clegg to the end of the war?
4 What other people might you expect to have had similar feelings to Rifleman Clegg?
5 If people felt like Rifleman Clegg, how do you explain the scenes in source F?

THE LOCOMOTIVE OF HISTORY

What were the effects of the First World War?

The First World War was not like previous wars. It involved the whole population. Everyone, in a sense, was in the front line. Everyone was affected. But did these changes outlast the war? Or did everything go back to the way it had been before the war?

Women – back in the cage?

A December 1918. Women vote for the first time.

B Girls on motorbikes, 1925. Before the war girls would never have been seen dressed like this. It would also have been considered quite improper for them to smoke in public.

Before the war a middle-class woman's place had been the home. Women were considered to be a fragile species, in need of protection by and from men. Many working-class women had to go to work, but mainly in domestic service.

The war had given many women the opportunity to work for the first time. Perhaps more importantly it had given women the chance to work in jobs that previously had been reserved for men. However, once the war was over men returned from the war and expected their jobs back. There was also no need for a massive munitions industry. By 1921 only 31 per cent of women had a paid job. In 1911 this figure had been 32 per cent. But everything was not quite the same. The 1919 Sex Disqualification (Removal) Act allowed women to follow a career in medicine or the law. Furthermore, in 1918, women were at last allowed to vote, although they had to be aged 30 or more. It was not until 1928 that women were able to vote at 21, the same age as men.

Nevertheless, one major change was the social attitude to women. The war had seen single women able to go out on their own. They could smoke and drink in public. Skirts became shorter because women needed to be able to move easily at work. Young women in the 1920s did not return to pre-war behaviour. These young women were known as 'flappers'. They wore trousers and behaved like men.

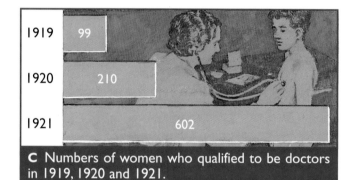

1919	99
1920	210
1921	602

C Numbers of women who qualified to be doctors in 1919, 1920 and 1921.

The government

During the war the government had been forced to take great control of the lives of ordinary people. The government had run major sections of the economy, such as the railways and the mines, not to mention the powerful Ministry of Munitions. With the war over, the government abandoned most of these roles. The railways and mines were handed back to their owners. Most of the war ministries also ceased to exist. Those that survived no longer had their original function. During the war the Ministry of Labour had been able to direct the nation's workforce. After the war it was simply put in charge of unemployment.

In the short term things returned to pre-war ways. In the longer term the way the government was organised during the First World War provided a model for government in the Second World War. It would not take two years for conscription to be introduced the second time around.

In May 1915 the Liberal Prime Minister had abandoned single party government and formed a coalition with the other two main parties. This became the standard way for dealing with the crises which Britain faced in the first half of the twentieth century. A National Government was formed in 1931 to deal with the Depression. The Second World War also saw Britain governed by a coalition government.

Trade unions

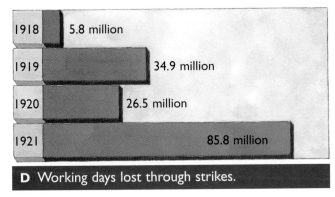

1918	5.8 million
1919	34.9 million
1920	26.5 million
1921	85.8 million

D Working days lost through strikes.

During the war the trade union leaders had accepted dilution and the large numbers of women who took men's jobs. Many workers had been unhappy that the leaders no longer represented their interests and so had elected shop stewards. These shop stewards were far more likely to call strikes than the official leaders, and they did not disappear once the war was over. The war had seen prices rise by 125 per cent. With peace, prices continued to rise. Workers now felt free to go on strike. They could no longer be accused of putting the country at risk. They wanted higher wages to cope with the rising prices.

The miners and the railway workers hoped for more than higher wages. They hoped that the government would not hand their industries back to their private owners. They liked working for a **nationalised industry**, that is, one which was owned by the government. They felt that private owners did not look after the safety of the workers or pay enough money. They believed that the government would treat the workers much better.

Debt

The war had cost Britain £9 million. Only 28 per cent of this had been paid for by taxation. The rest had been borrowed. The government could not afford to pay this back. This was called the National Debt. It was 14 times greater in 1919 than it had been before the war. Half of all the money raised from taxes went just to pay off the interest on this debt. This meant that the government

"OLIVER 'ASKS' FOR MORE."

E A cartoon from *Punch*, April 1920. The miners are shown demanding more money from the Prime Minister, Lloyd George. *Miner (holding the bowl and the club):* 'You'll be sorry one of these days that you didn't give me nationalisation.' *Lloyd George:* 'If you keep on like this there won't be any nation left to nationalise you.'

could not afford to build the 600 000 new houses that had been promised. The government needed a growing British economy to produce more taxation. But in 1920–21 the British economy slumped. Unemployment grew and so income from taxes declined.

1 Look at source E. How are the miners shown as threatening the government?
2 Does source D support this opinion?
3 The miner in the cartoon says that the government will regret not nationalising the mines. What does he mean by nationalisation and why did he want it?

Extended writing
Trotsky, the Russian communist leader, said 'War is the locomotive of history'. He meant that war speeds up change and makes things happen much more quickly. Is this true of the First World War? Look at how the war affected:
a) political life – the role of the government and political parties.
b) social attitudes – did attitudes to the role of women change?
c) economic life – was Britain still a prosperous country?

5

The New Women?

How did women win the right to vote? What changes were there in the role and status of women in the first half of the twentieth century?

Votes for women

At the beginning of the twentieth century no woman could vote. For that matter the only men who could vote were those who owned their own house. In the nineteenth century the National Union of Women's Suffrage Societies (NUWSS) had been set up to demand the vote for women. It was mainly supported by women who had good jobs or were wealthy. The NUWSS was led by Millicent Fawcett and by 1914 had become a large organisation of 53 000 members. The NUWSS's main concern was to get the vote for women on the same terms as men. In other words it was not campaigning for all adults to have the vote, only those who owned houses. The members of the NUWSS were commonly known as Suffragists.

Another group wanted votes for women, not just house owners. In 1903 Emmeline Pankhurst, the daughter of a wealthy cotton manufacturer, set up the Women's Suffrage and Political Union (WSPU), whose members were more usually known as Suffragettes. Their slogan was 'Deeds not Words'. The WSPU engaged in **direct action**. They disrupted political meetings, chained themselves to railings, slashed paintings in the National Gallery and even planted a small bomb in Westminster Abbey. The purpose was to gain people's attention.

Such actions were very shocking in an age when a woman's main purpose was to get married and then obey her husband. The most famous protest occurred in 1913 when Emily Davison ran out in front of the King's horse during the Derby. Her funeral was watched by a large audience and her death created enormous publicity. But despite all the publicity women were still not given the vote. MPs who agreed with votes for women introduced bills into parliament in 1907, 1908 and twice in 1910 but they were all defeated. While some Conservative MPs agreed with the demands of the Suffragists, only the Labour Party supported the Suffragettes.

A A comment by the Liberal MP W R Cremer, in 1907.

At a Parliamentary Election there would be about one million more women electors and they would swamp the male electors whenever they chose to do so.

B A comment in the *Daily Mirror*, 1906.

When the Suffragettes began their campaign they were mistaken for notoriety hunters, featherheads, flibbertigibbets. Their proceedings were not taken seriously. Now they have proved they are in dead earnest, they have frightened the Government, they have broken the law, they have made votes for women practical politics.

The First World War

The breakthrough came with the outbreak of war. Campaigners wanted women to be able to prove their worth by helping the war effort. The London branch of the NUWSS used its organisation to train women to take on jobs previously held by men. They set up training classes in oxyacetylene welding as well as munitions work. But the Suffragettes were divided. The majority, led by Emmeline Pankhurst and her daughter Christabel, supported the war because it would give women a chance to prove that they were as good as men. They demanded the 'Right to Serve', so that women could play a full part in the war effort. In July 1915 30 000 Suffragette supporters took part in a march to demand the 'Right to Serve'. Emmeline's other daughter, Sylvia, opposed this point of view. She believed that women should not support a government that women had not been able to vote for.

The majority view, however, seemed to have got it right. Many thousands of women joined up as nurses in the Voluntary Aid Detachments (VADs) while others worked in factories and in other jobs (see page 28). Women were able to use the war to prove that they could play a full part in the life of the country. The result was a partial victory. The Representation of the People Act of 1918 gave the vote to all women who were over the age of 30 and who also owned a house or were married to a house owner. In the 1918 general election Countess Markiewicz became the first woman to be elected to parliament, although along with the other 72 Sinn Fein MPs she refused to take up her

'Ever since the world was created, most women have been of weaker mental power than men with a tendency to submit to the control of the stronger sex.' This is how *The Times* reacted in 1867 when it was suggested women be allowed to vote.

seat as a protest against the English refusal to grant independence to Ireland. But it was not until 1928 that all women over the age of 21 were given the vote, exactly the same qualification as had been given to men in 1918.

E Charles Graves, writing in 1922.

The Vote was won, not by burning churches, mutilating pictures, or damaging pillar boxes but by women's work during the war. It was not a concession to violence but an acknowledgement of patriotic service.

F In 1929 Margaret Bondfield became the first ever woman cabinet minister. She was made Minister of Labour in the second Labour government.

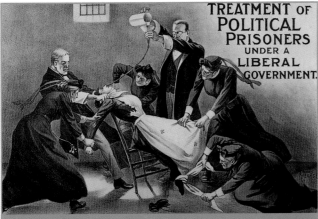

C This poster was issued by the Suffragettes. Suffragettes who were imprisoned for their activities sometimes went on hunger strike. The poster shows a hunger striker being force-fed.

Q

1 Look at sources A and D. How do they help to explain why it took so long for women to be granted the vote?
2 What other reasons can you find to explain why women were not given the vote until 1918?
3 What was the 'patriotic service' referred to in source E?
4 Does the writer of source E believe that the activities of the Suffragettes before the war secured the vote for women? Explain your answer.
5 Which source supports the view of source E and which source disagrees with it? Which view do you agree with?

Extended writing 'Do you think that the campaign of the Suffragettes won the vote for women?' To answer this question try to work out which of the three factors below was the most important in gaining the vote for women:
a) the Suffragists   b) the Suffragettes
c) the First World War.

For each of the three find evidence to show their influence. Then decide which is the most important and explain your decision using the evidence you have found.

"What's the disturbance in the market place?"
"It's a mass meeting of the women who've changed their minds since this morning and want to alter their voting papers."

D A cartoon from the English magazine *Punch*, 18 December 1918. What does this tell you about men's attitudes to women in 1918?

WOMEN AND WORK

Women's work at the start of the century

At the beginning of the century most women did not have paid work. The government census of 1911 revealed that over 11 million adult women did not have a paid job, in contrast to fewer than five million women who did. The reason for this was that women were expected to marry and become housewives. Their job was to care for their husbands and bring up a family. Women grew up accepting that men earned the money for the family. Women were dependent upon men. They grew up in a household dominated by men, and then they left to get married, once more to be dominated by the man.

For working-class women, the commonest jobs were as servants and cooks. This was known as 'going into service'. Although some servants were married, service was considered to be especially suitable for a young woman because it taught her the skills that she would need to be a housewife. In other words, even working-class husbands expected their wives to give up their jobs once they were married. Many men did not consider it to be respectable to send their wives out to work. Even though it meant the family having to survive

B Women working in a hat factory in Manchester in 1909.

on little money, this was considered to be better than having a wife who worked. Her role was to look after the family. However, some working-class women did not have a choice about working. Their husbands did not earn enough and so wives had to have a paid job as well as being a housewife.

In the industrial areas of Britain in the north and midlands many women worked in factories. Once more the majority of those who worked were unmarried women, although married women were allowed to work in factories. The Lancashire textile mills were famous for employing large numbers of women. Indeed the percentage of Lancashire working-class women with a job was about the same in 1900 as it is today. Throughout the country many poor women also worked in what were known as the 'sweated' trades, such as hat and dress-making. They were forced to work long hours for little money. Even so, the majority of working-class women didn't have a job. Those who did were paid far less than men.

A Women shelling peas in Covent Garden, London. This was one of the worst paid jobs.

C Enid Starkie, writing in 1941, remembers her childhood at the turn of the century (from *A Lady's Child*).

My father seemed to me to be a very important person … In my mother's opinion everything he did was right … She considered it right that the life of a wife, that the life of all women in the household, should revolve around its male head. Nurse, the maids and even Lizzie the cook, accepted this attitude without question.

D Boys and girls at an elementary school at the start of the century.

Middle-class girls might work as shop assistants or in an office, but they were expected to give up the job as soon as they got married. Indeed some jobs, such as teaching and bank work, demanded this. However, women were paid much less than men, even when they were doing similar work.

Although the life of a middle-class woman did not include a job it had many benefits. Her house would have been full of servants to do the cooking and the cleaning. This left women with a great deal of time to do other things, such as play tennis or visit friends. A wife and daughters with lots of time on their hands was a sign of status for a middle-class family. Things were not the same for working-class wives. Even those who had a job still had to feed the family and keep the house clean despite having little money. Cleanliness was seen as a sign of respectability. The front step of the house was kept spotlessly clean as an outward sign of this.

By 1900 boys and girls received a similar basic schooling. However, far more boys than girls were likely to go on to secondary school. Just a very few rich girls went to university. In the 1850s Millicent Fawcett's sister, Elizabeth Garrett Anderson, had been refused the chance to become a medical student. Although her example eventually led to women training to be doctors, there were still only 260 in the whole of Britain in 1900.

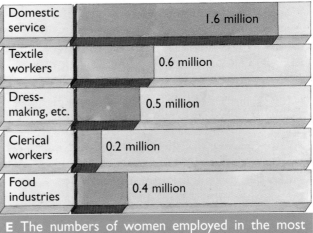

Domestic service	1.6 million
Textile workers	0.6 million
Dress-making, etc.	0.5 million
Clerical workers	0.2 million
Food industries	0.4 million

E The numbers of women employed in the most common occupations for women in 1911.

Q

1 Look at source E. Which was the most common job for women in 1911?
2 Why was this?
3 What reasons can you find to explain why most women did not work in 1911?
4 What examples can you find to show that women were not treated the same as men at the beginning of the twentieth century? What reasons can you think of to explain this?

WOMEN AND THE FIRST WORLD WAR

Key Issue **How did the First World War affect the lives and status of women?**

The war offered many women great opportunities for work. In 1915 the Marchioness of Londonderry set up the Women's Legion, which organised more than 40 000 women to work as cooks and nurses in the army and so allow more men to go and fight. Even more successful were the Voluntary Aid Detachments (VADs). These had been set up in 1910 to provide more nurses for the army. They were open to both men and women but in the event it was mainly women who joined up, with over 15 000 volunteering during the war.

There was no pay and so only women from reasonably well-off families could join the VADs. Many of them had little idea of what awaited them. Vera Brittain, who served in the VADs, remarked that women 'came to the hospital expecting to hold the patients' hands and smooth their pillows while regular nurses fetched and carried everything that looked and smelt disagreeable'. The reality was very different. Even though the VADs were stationed well behind the front lines, they had to work long hours and look after men who were in constant pain and suffering from terrible wounds. However, for many middle and upper-class women the VADs provided the first ever opportunity to leave home and become independent people. In the main working-class women had to seek their opportunities for war work on the home front (see pages 30–31).

B A poster to encourage women to join the VADs.

The first VAD unit left for France in October 1914. But the VADs were not only nurses. In 1915 the scheme was extended by the creation of the VAD General Section. This organised women to carry out such jobs as cooks, clerks and accountants. The idea was to free men from these jobs so that they could fight in the front line. It also provided an opportunity for those women who didn't want to become nurses.

The Two Madonnas of Pervyse

For some women even the VADs were not enough. Elsie Knocker and Mairi Chisholm had gone to Belgium to work as nurses in a hospital but had realised that many men with non-critical injuries were dying of shock long before they reached the hospital. Therefore the two women set up their own first aid post right behind the front lines in the Belgian town of Pervyse. For three and a half years they tended the wounded, until they were caught up in a German gas attack and had to be sent back to England. They were named the Two Madonnas of Pervyse by the local people, and they were awarded the Military Medal by the British army.

A VAD drivers stand ready by their ambulances in France in 1917.

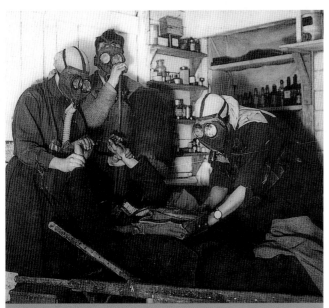

C The two Madonnas give artificial respiration to a soldier during a gas attack. A Belgian orderly helps out in the background.

D Mairi Chisholm describes what it was like being a front-line nurse, in an oral interview in 1976:

We slept with our clothes on – at any moment you'd hear a roar of 'blessés, blessés, blessés' [wounded men] and the door would be flung open and the soldiers would bring in one of their companions. And also we went out into the trenches a lot ourselves, and poked our noses around to see everybody was all right, and occasionally we went out into the advance trenches, which were within 25 yards of the Germans.

Although women could join the VADs and do various jobs, until 1917 they couldn't actually join the armed forces. In the first days of the war a voluntary organisation, the Women's Emergency Reserve, had been formed. This later changed its name to the Women's Volunteer Reserve. It provided volunteers to run canteens and ambulances for the troops, as well as raising money to provide facilities for them. However, although it had a uniform it was not an official group. The armed forces were not considered to be a place for women.

This view began to change with the terrible casualties being suffered, especially after the Battle of the Somme. In 1917 all three services set up women's sections: the Women's Army Auxiliary Corps (WAAC), the Women's Royal Naval Service (WRNS) and the Women's Royal Air Force (WRAF). These sections employed over 100 000 women as drivers, typists and cooks. The army needed to send every possible fighting man to the front, and having women carrying out the non-combatant jobs allowed them to do this.

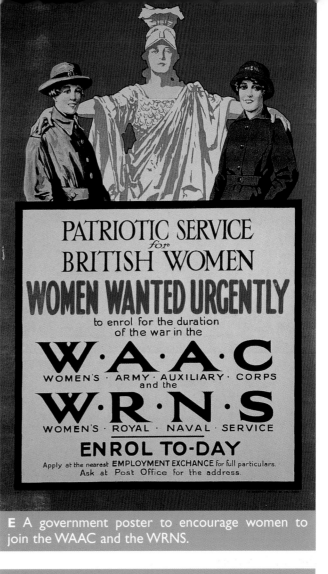

E A government poster to encourage women to join the WAAC and the WRNS.

F A book produced by the government in 1918 describes the purpose of the WAACs.

Each cook replaces one man, while among the clerks at present the ratio is four women to three men. Every WAAC who goes to France is like the pawn who attains the top of the chessboard and is exchanged for a more valuable piece. She sends a fighting man to his job by taking all the jobs that are really a woman's after all. For is it not woman's earliest job to look after man?

Q

1 Look at source B. Do you think it was produced before or after 1915? Why do you think this?
2 Look at source A and read source D. What image of women do they give?
3 What evidence can you find which shows that men were impressed by these women?
4 What evidence can you find which suggests that women were still not regarded as equal by men?

WOMEN ON THE HOME FRONT

A Women in the fire brigade. The war offered women jobs in areas that had previously only been available to men.

B 'For King and Country'. This painting was produced during the war by E F Skinner and shows women working in a munitions factory.

C A government poster to encourage women to become workers in munitions factories.

In July 1915 Christabel Pankhurst led a march of 30 000 women who demanded 'The Right to Serve'. This was soon granted. In January 1916 conscription was introduced. No longer could the army rely on volunteers. Men would be ordered to join up. This meant that there was a need for women to fill the jobs which were being left by the men. Quite often these were jobs which had never been done by women. Women became conductors on buses and trams, though very few were allowed to become drivers. (Drivers were paid more than conductors. Men were worried that if women became drivers it would cause their wages to be reduced.) Women were also allowed to join the police for the first time. They became chimney sweeps and ran bakeries. As early as 1916 every London ambulance was driven by a woman. Nearly 750 000 women took jobs as clerks, and while this type of job had been filled by women before the war, they had never done so in such huge numbers.

Canaries

Sometimes the trains were packed, so of course the porters knew that we were all munitions kids, and they'd say, 'Go on girl, 'op in there', and they would open the first class carriages … Of course conductors used to say on the trains 'you'll die in two years, cock.' So we said, 'We don't mind dying for our country.' We were so young we didn't realise.

The change rooms were fearfully crowded, long troughs were provided instead of wash basins, and there is always a scarcity of soap and towels. The girls' danger clothes are often horribly dirty and in rags … Although the fumes often meant 16 or 18 casualties a night there were only four beds for men and women and they are all in the same room.

Not every job filled by a woman was as a replacement for a man. In 1915 the army blamed its defeats on a lack of artillery shells. The British people were horrified to think that soldiers might be dying simply because the government was not doing its job properly. The result of this was a huge increase in the production of shells by private companies. New jobs were created in these munitions factories, and by the end of the war over 900 000 women had filled them.

However, this was very dangerous work. Explosions could kill and maim the workers. The chemicals used in the explosives caused workers to vomit and eventually turned their skin yellow, earning them the nickname of canaries.

Nevertheless, munitions work was very well paid, often twice as much as working as a servant. In some cases a munitions worker could earn as much as five pounds a week. Therefore many working-class women were willing to do this work.

Khaki fever

Before the war, unmarried middle and upper-class girls would always have been chaperoned – usually by an older female relative. The war gave much greater freedom to women, especially single women. By going out to work they could now meet men on their own. This freedom changed some attitudes. It was now more acceptable for women to smoke and drink in public. However,

the war also saw a great increase in illegitimate births. Any girl who had a baby outside marriage was considered to be immoral. At a time when birth control was not available to ordinary people many girls were forced to have illegal abortions. Some died from these.

… girls used to come to me saying 'I'm going to have a baby … I can go to Bradford.' They could get an illegal operation there – well it was an illegal operation then. I've a few five quids [pounds] that I've given out to girls. They didn't have it done in Leeds because they were frightened of somebody getting to know.

After the war

When the war ended many women lost their jobs. Men returned to claim back their former jobs. Many other jobs disappeared. There was no need to produce huge quantities of armaments. There were fewer jobs in domestic service. By 1921 the economic decline meant that the number of women in work was actually lower than in 1911. However, in 1919 the Sex Disqualification (Removal) Act was passed. This opened up professional careers to women, allowing them to become barristers, vets and higher civil servants, as well as allowing them to become police officers with the same powers as men (only certain areas of the country had allowed women to become police officers during the war).

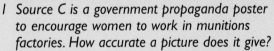

1 Source C is a government propaganda poster to encourage women to work in munitions factories. How accurate a picture does it give?
2 Source B is an official painting. Compare it to the description in source E. In what ways do they differ? Why do you think this is?
3 Read source D. How were munitions workers regarded by other people?

Extended writing
'The First World War led to great change in the role of women in Britain.' Using the sources on pages 26–31 and your own knowledge, comment on whether you agree or disagree with this interpretation.

WOMEN AND THE SECOND WORLD WAR

A A 'Balloon Site, Coventry', by Dame Laura Knight. This is an official painting.

Between the wars

During the Depression of the 1930s (see pages 42–47) women who had jobs came under a great deal of pressure. They were seen as taking jobs from men. When a man was unemployed it was seen as a serious problem. It was not thought to be so important if a woman was unemployed. Her main role was still seen as being a housewife. Therefore it was government policy to keep married women out of jobs like teaching. It meant that there were more jobs for men.

While some young women now wore their skirts short and smoked in public, life for most ordinary women was not really very different. Girls were still brought up not to compete with boys. Abortion was still a criminal offence and many restaurants would still not serve a woman who did not have a man with her.

War breaks out

When war broke out in 1939 the armed services once more set up women's forces as they had done in the First World War: Women's Royal Naval Service, (Wrens), the Women's Auxiliary Airforce (WAAF) and the Auxiliary Territorial Services (ATS) in the army. However, to begin with the government did not exactly encourage women to join up. In 1939 the Ministry of Information announced that women should not join up unless they had special qualifications. The rest should stay at home and look after the country's nine million children and six million elderly. But all this changed once Hitler's armies had overrun Europe. The government realised it needed to get as many women as possible into the factories. Munitions factories sprang up throughout the country. With the Battle of Britain and the Blitz Britain's fate depended on making enough planes to stop the German airforce. Women in the aircraft industry found themselves working an unbelievable 112 hours a week. Yet women were still not rewarded with the same pay as men, nor the same level of compensation if they were injured.

B The shortage of women volunteers according to the *Evening Standard*, 13 March 1941.

A fair proportion of married women have children and may be unwilling to volunteer until they have made arrangements for their care. Ministry of Labour local welfare officers are recommending local authorities to establish day nurseries.

C A middle-class housewife from Bradford comments on her treatment by male officers during her time in the ATS during the war.

The officers seem to think that if a girl speaks with a northern accent she is … a barbarian and proceed to treat her as if she were a kitchen maid.

D A Wren cleaning the shoes of naval officers.

Conscription

By September 1941 three million women had registered for war work of one type or another. This was not enough. With seven and a half million men called up, more women were needed to replace them. Therefore in December 1941 the government introduced conscription for women for the first time ever. All single women between the ages of 19 and 40 were conscripted to play a part in the war. They could choose between serving in one of the services or working in industrial production. In fact two thirds of the women called up chose to join the services. But this meant there were still not enough women in industry and so the age of conscription was raised to 51 and young mothers were also brought into work. By 1943 there were over seven million women taking part in war-related work.

Women found themselves driving lorries, sweeping chimneys, unloading ships' cargoes, repairing gas mains and working with the fire brigade as well as many other jobs. As in the First World War, many became nurses and were sent all over the world, as well as working on the home front. Girls who joined the ATS and other services could do so from the age of 17. Many had been living at home and so joining up gave them the chance to escape from their parents for the first time. The ATS also gave women their only chance for front line fighting. Some women were allowed to join the crews of the anti-aircraft guns which fired at the German bombers. This was dangerous and 335 ATS members were killed in such action. The WAAFs also operated barrage balloons, as shown in source A. These balloons had cables attached which forced the German bombers to fly too high for accurate bombing.

When the war was over the men once more came home to their old jobs. However, everything did not return to the way it had been before. Many more married women were in work in 1951 than had been the case before the war. The 1944 Education Act finally allowed married women to teach, although they did not receive the same pay as men.

F Anne Valery had been a member of the ATS. She remembers how she was treated by a man in 1947.

> I have the bitter memory of being a passenger in a car that had broken down, and of suggesting that … there was dirt in the carburettor. The driver chose not to hear me, fetching a mechanic who took half an hour to discover that the fault was just that. Biting back 'I told you so', I kept quiet, for two years of peace had taught me my place.

1914	Men	£94
	Women	£50
1936	Men	£186
	Women	£104
1956	Men	£634
	Women	£319

G Average earnings in Britain.

Q

1 What reasons can you find which might explain why not enough women volunteered before September 1941?
2 Look at source G. What does this source tell you about women's wages between 1911 and 1951?

Extended writing
Did the role and status of women really change between 1918 and 1951? Use the evidence from pages 32–33 to back up your answer.
  You should refer to the following:
  a) women's political opportunities
  b) women's job opportunities
  c) social attitude to women
  d) changes for women in the two World Wars
  e) how long lasting these changes were.

E Women prepare to ladle molten steel at a steel-works.

6

Britain after the First World War – 'A fit land for heroes'?

Why was Britain not rich enough to create a 'fit land for heroes' after the end of the war?

The First World War came to an end at 11 am on the eleventh day of the eleventh month of 1918. Lloyd George immediately called a general election. He wanted the British people to allow him and his coalition of Liberals and Conservatives to stay in power. They had won the war. Now they promised the British people that they would create 'a fit land for heroes to live in'. Everyone expected that peace would bring prosperity. The Labour Party left the coalition and were the only real opposition to the government in the election. The government won 526 seats while Labour won 63. It was a huge victory for Lloyd George.

The post-war boom

The end of the war did not immediately result in high unemployment for the returning soldiers. Many of the women who had worked during the war now lost their jobs to men. An economic boom created jobs for the rest. People had been unable to spend much money during the war

A
A Labour Party poster from 1923. It was issued along with the poster in source B.

years and so had built up savings. Now they wanted to be able to buy the sorts of things which had been unavailable during the war. Also, France and Belgium needed British goods because so much of their own industry had been destroyed in the war. However, the boom did not last for long. By 1921 unemployment had reached almost two million.

B The other half of the Labour poster campaign.

Depression in the 1920s

Why was it that the boom was so short-lived? There were two main reasons for this.

1 Competition

Britain's exports grew, but not every industry enjoyed this expansion. The traditional industries of Britain, such as coal and textiles, faced new competition from countries which produced the same goods more cheaply. For example, India used to be a major market for British-produced cotton goods. In the 1920s India began to buy cotton goods from Japan. By 1935 it was buying more from Japan than from Britain.

2 The collapse of world trade

Before the war Britain had been the world's major trading nation. Its prosperity depended on world trade expanding. However, world trade declined. There was far less trade between European countries. Much of the industry of France and

Belgium had been destroyed in the war. This meant they were producing fewer goods for export and so they were able to buy less from other countries, such as Britain. Germany had to pay such a huge amount in reparations that it could not afford to buy so many British goods.

The problem was not confined to Europe. Europe was not able to buy as much from other countries around the world. It bought less beef from Argentina and less grain from Canada, for example. This meant that Argentina and Canada couldn't afford to buy from Britain. Less trade also meant there was less demand for ships, and so this produced unemployment in Britain's shipyards.

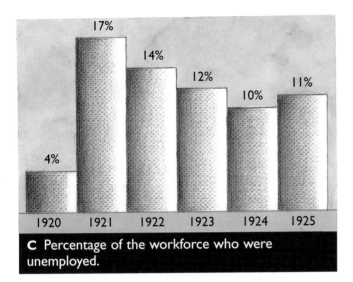

C Percentage of the workforce who were unemployed.

The return to the Gold Standard

In 1925 the government decided to return to the Gold Standard. This meant that the pound was now worth a fixed amount of gold, equivalent to $4.86. Returning to the Gold Standard gave the impression that the pound was once again the most important currency in the world. However, setting its value at such a high level had disadvantages. It meant that British exports became more expensive, making it more difficult for British companies to sell their goods abroad. Britain was already facing competition from countries like Germany and Japan. Returning to the Gold Standard made the problem worse.

'Little better than a pig sty'

Walter Long, the President of the Local Government Board, promised to build homes worthy of the returning heroes. 'To let them [the soldiers] come home from horrible water-logged trenches to something little better than a pig sty here would, indeed, be criminal.' In 1919 Lloyd George's government began to make good this promise. It introduced a law which required all

towns with more than 20 000 inhabitants to build council housing. The government would help by paying some of the building costs. The housing could then be rented to poorer people. The houses would have lavatories, running water and a kitchen. Over the next three years 200 000 new houses were built. These were a huge improvement on the pre-war slums, but they were not enough.

D A slum in Nottingham. This was the sort of housing that the government was promising to replace. This photograph was taken in 1931.

The Geddes Axe

The trade slump in 1921 caused real problems for the government. More people out of work meant that there were less people paying tax. So the government had less money to spend. The government set up a committee under Sir Eric Geddes. Its job was to find ways to cut government spending. These cuts were introduced in 1922 and were known as the 'Geddes Axe'. Spending on defence and education was cut. The scheme to build new houses was also abandoned. Very few heroes would get a new home. Not only that, but the government also cut unemployment benefit. This was not the promised 'fit land for heroes'.

Q

1 What point was the Labour Party making with sources A and B?
2 Why were British workers facing such hardships by 1923? You will need to consider:
   a) the collapse of world trade
   b) foreign competition
   c) Geddes axe.

7

The General Strike – Nine Days' Wonder

Why was there a General Strike in 1926?
Who won the General Strike?

In 1926 Britain was rocked by a General Strike. Many British workers refused to work. They did this in support of the miners, who had had their wages cut. But after just nine days the strike ended. The miners did not have their wages raised. They stayed out on strike on their own. In the end poverty forced them to give in and go back to work for lower wages. Why did the General Strike happen and why did it end so quickly?

The coal industry before the General Strike

During the First World War the government had taken control of the coalmines in order to make sure that the country would have enough coal. In 1921 the mines were handed back to their owners. But since the First World War coal prices had fallen. This meant that the coalmine owners were not making as much profit as they used to. They therefore wanted to cut the wages of the miners, who were already poorly paid. This would help the owners to make more money.

The mines were to be handed back to the owners on 31 March 1921. Before this date the mine owners announced the cut in miners' wages. The miners refused to accept the cuts and so on 31 March they were locked out of the mines. The miners were supported by the two other main trade unions, the railway workers and the transport workers. Together the three unions formed the 'Triple Alliance'. If they all went on strike at the same time they could stop the country's economy. The Triple Alliance was meant to strike in support of the miners on 16 April. On 15 April the other two unions backed down. The miners felt betrayed and they eventually lost the strike.

B An extract from the *Graphic* in April 1921:

American coal … can be mined cheaply because it is near the surface and in thick, easily worked seams … British coal is hard to obtain because it is very deep, often in thin seams.

C A miner describes conditions in a mine in 1914.

What a collier [miner] could do by working hard all day, this machine [a coal cutter] would accomplish in two minutes … the drawback was in the added danger, because you could not hear the roof cracking, and with such a large undercut there was the likelihood of it falling any second.

A Working underground at Frog Lane Pit, Bristol, 1905. Miners had to work in dangerous and cramped conditions. The only safety measures were the wooden pit props which supported the roof.

287 million tons

267 million tons

238 million tons

1913   1924   1928

D Coal production between 1913 and 1928.

E Miners' pickets in the 1921 strike. These miners were protesting at wage cuts.

In 1923–4 profits in the coal industry improved and wages rose once more. But by 1925 cheap coal from Germany was undercutting British coal. Also, most of the easily mined coal had been used up in the First World War and this meant that as time went on, British miners were having to mine coal which was more expensive to extract. The mine owners decided to cut miners' wages once again.

The Miners' Federation were regarded as the strongest union in the country. Other workers were worried that if the Miners' Federation could not protect the wages of the miners then it would not be long before the wages of most other workers were also cut. This meant that other unions wanted to help the miners to win their struggle by going on strike as well. On 'Red Friday', 31 July 1925, a General Strike was threatened when the mine owners announced cuts in miners' wages.

The government did not want the strike to happen. Therefore they agreed to top up the miners' wages. This meant that the mine owners cut the money they paid to the miners, but the government made up the difference. The miners still got the same amount of money. The government agreed to do this for nine months. At the same time the government set up a Royal Commission to look at the coal industry and suggest a solution to the problem.

In 1926 the Commission made its report. It recommended improvements in the working and living conditions of the miners but also said that wages had to be cut. The Miners' Federation rejected the report. They asked for the support of the other trade unions. The General Council of the **Trades Union Congress** (TUC) called for a General Strike which began on 3 May. Over two million workers joined the strike. Printers, rail and bus workers and dockers all stopped work. The TUC hoped that the strike would create so many problems for the owners of other industries that they would force the government and the mine owners to give in. Essential services such as refuse collectors were not asked to join so that the public health was not put at risk. Oddly enough, one group not on strike were the miners. They had been locked out of the mines by the owners because they wouldn't accept the pay cuts.

Q

1 Look at source D. What problem facing the coal industry does it show?
2 What other problems were faced by the coal industry after the First World War?
3 Why did the miners go on strike in 1926?
4 Why did the other unions support them?
5 Look at sources A and C. How do they help you to understand why miners were not willing to accept a cut in their pay?

THE NINE DAYS

While the strike lasted it received great support from union members. However, the country did not entirely grind to a halt. The armed forces made sure that food got to the shops. Anti-strike volunteers helped to run public transport. On 11 May Sir Herbert Samuel, who had chaired the Royal Commission, offered to help to solve the strike. On 12 May the TUC General Council accepted his ideas, which included pay cuts for the miners. The strike was over. The miners continued to hold out but without the support of the other unions they had little chance of success. They had no wages coming in and so in December 1926 they finally accepted defeat.

THE LEVER BREAKS.

B 'The lever breaks.' A cartoon in the magazine *Punch*, 19 May 1926. This magazine was read largely by the middle class. It supported the employers during the General Strike.

A The front page of the *Illustrated London News*, 15 May 1926, shows a food convoy protected by armoured vehicles travelling down the East India Dock Road in London during the General Strike.

C Workers at the *Daily Mail* refused to print this editorial attacking the strikers on 3 May 1926.

The general strike is not an industrial dispute; it is a revolutionary movement, intended to inflict suffering on the great mass of innocent persons in the community, and thereby put pressure on the government.

D An extract from *The British Worker*, 10 May 1926. With the printers on strike there were no daily papers being produced. However, workers on the *Daily Herald* produced *The British Worker* to get the strikers' message across.

A procession of transport workers, be-medalled and in Sunday clothes, marched in fours to Brockwell Park. The immense crowd in the park gave a clear indication of where the sympathies of the British nation lie in this dispute. Many of the crowd were Trade Unionists, including strikers and their families. But at least a third of them were of a class which the press loves to call 'the general public' – bank and insurance clerks, small shopkeepers, holders of season tickets, dwellers in suburban villas.

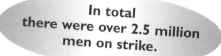

In total there were over 2.5 million men on strike.

F The *Daily Express*, 7 May 1926.

The Trades Union Congress with perfect truth define the issue as *for or against the strike. The vast majority of the nation including most of the strikers are against it.* The British public are on the side of Parliamentary government.

G 'It aint gonna reign no more.' A J Cook was the Secretary of the Miners' Federation.

E Volunteer train drivers and firemen proudly pose in front of an engine.

Q

1 Is source F right? Did the majority of British people oppose the strike? What evidence can you find about how people felt?
2 What opinion of the miners is given by the cartoonist in source G? How does he show this in the cartoon?
3 Which other sources agree with the opinion shown in source G?
4 Which sources disagree with this opinion?
5 Which opinion do you agree with? Explain your answer.

WHO WERE THE LOSERS IN THE GENERAL STRIKE?

Although the Trades Union Congress had pulled out of the strike, the miners did not give up the struggle for many months. They felt betrayed by the TUC. Why did the General Strike last just nine days?

One important reason is that the leaders of the TUC were divided. Some believed that going on strike would bring success. Others felt that since Taff Vale (see page 6), strikes could not work. They felt that the miners must make a deal with the owners. Half of the General Council of the TUC were also MPs. They were very afraid that ordinary people would look on the strikers as revolutionaries. After all, this is how papers like the *Daily Mail* and the *Daily Express* showed them (see pages 38–39). These Labour MPs were frightened that the public would also think of the Labour Party as revolutionary. It was only in 1924 that Labour had formed its first ever government. If middle-class voters thought of Labour as a party that wanted to destroy parliament it would never again be elected to form another government.

A A statement issued in January 1927 by the Miners' Federation.

> If we were deserted and forced to fight a lone fight, it was not by the workers that we were abandoned. Their hearts beat true to the end ... On Tuesday evening, the 11th of May, The Miners' Executive were sent for by the General Council and were informed that they [the Council] had agreed upon and accepted proposals as the outcome of conversations between their officials and Sir Herbert Samuel.

The aftermath of the strike

The miners stayed out on strike. The mine owners realised they were going to win and so they refused to compromise. By October and November many miners were so poor that they had no choice. They had to go back to work. When they returned to work the miners were forced to accept longer hours and lower wages. At first sight it looks as though the miners were the losers along with the TUC, while the government and the mine owners were the clear winners. However, is it really that simple?

In 1927 the government passed the Trade Disputes and Trade Union Act. This made it illegal for unions to hold sympathy strikes on behalf of other workers. In other words general strikes were made illegal. In the years before 1926 about one million workers a year went on strike. In the years after 1926 this figure fell to 300 000. However, this was largely because the union movement was controlled by leaders such as Ernest Bevin, who did not believe in going on strike.

B The British historian A J P Taylor writing in 1965 (*British History 1914–45*).

> In the end, the owners were destroyed by their victory. The class war continued in the coal districts when it was fading elsewhere, and the miners insisted on nationalisation as soon as power passed into their hands [the Labour victory in 1945].

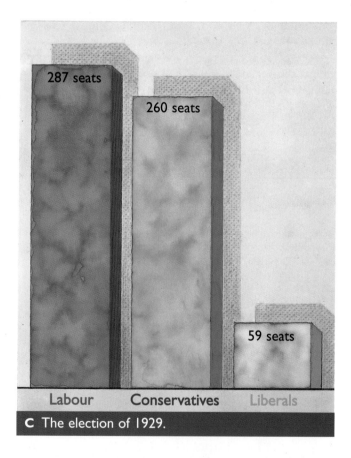

287 seats

260 seats

59 seats

Labour   Conservatives   Liberals

C The election of 1929.

D The view of Margaret Morris, a British historian, writing in 1994:

> Although there was a breach between many of the rank and file trade unionists and the official leaders, the Trade Disputes Act brought the unions and the Labour Party close together and helped to produce the election of the 1929 Labour government.

E Unemployed miners in the Welsh village of Pontypridd in the 1930s. They have cleared a hillside of stones to create allotments so that they can grow some food to eat.

1924   1928   1933   1938

F Miners employed in the coal industry.

Q

1 Source B suggests that the mine owners lost the General Strike. Do you agree with this interpretation? Explain your answer using the evidence from this unit to support your views.

2 Who do you think were the winners and losers in the General Strike?
Fill in the table below.

Group	Evidence that suggests this group won	Evidence that suggests this group lost
Miners		
Mine owners		
TUC		
Government		

The Depression

**What were the effects of the Depression?
Did everyone suffer in the Depression?**

The second Labour government

In May 1929 the Labour Party won the general election and so Ramsay MacDonald formed a government for the second time. However, Labour did not have an overall majority. They needed the support of Liberal MPs to pass any new laws. Labour were able to introduce some reforms. For instance, they cut the working day in the mines from eight hours down to seven and a half hours and restarted the slum clearance programmme. But when they tried to abolish the Trades Disputes Act the Liberals stopped them. They did not want to see another General Strike.

This made governing the country difficult enough but worse was to follow. In October the economy was hit by the Great Depression. As

B A bar chart showing British unemployment.

A Ramsay MacDonald puts the cart before the horse. A cartoon from the *Evening Standard*, 30 November 1929. The phrase 'putting the cart before the horse' means that you are carrying out your actions in the wrong order. In this case the government first needed to get people back to work so that they could pay taxes to fund the social reforms.

unemployment spread in the USA so demand for goods dropped and British exports to America fell. A similar scene occurred in other European countries and so all trade declined, producing unemployment everywhere. This caused demand to fall still further and produced still more unemployment. Pages 34 and 35 explain why the fall in world trade caused high unemployment in Britain in the early 1920s. The Depression which began in 1929 was much worse. By 1932 unemployment had reached over 13 million in America and almost six million in Germany.

The government did try to create more jobs by investing in building projects. But the £42 million which was spent was far too little to make any difference. The government dared not risk more. One government minister who did want the government to do more was Oswald Mosley. He proposed raising import duties to protect British industries, increasing pensions and giving the government much more control over industry. When the government didn't follow his advice he resigned. He then went on to form a fascist party (see pages 48–49).

The crisis of 1931

The government had three serious problems by 1931.

1 Britain still needed to import large quantities of food. In the past the cost of this would be more than equalled by the value of the manufactured goods sold abroad. The collapse in trade meant that this was no longer the case. Britain was importing far more than it exported. This is known as a balance of trade deficit.
2 The pound was traditionally the world's major currency. However, with a balance of trade deficit the pound no longer seemed a strong currency. Currency speculators started a 'run on the pound'. This means they decided to sell their pounds and exchange them for gold. Britain needed to borrow money to support the pound, so that its gold reserves would not be used up.
3 Rising unemployment meant that the government got less money from taxes because only people with a job paid tax. At the same time the government had to pay out more money in unemployment benefit. The Labour government decided that the best way out of this problem was to cut unemployment benefit.They also decided to pay lower wages to people who worked for the government, such as civil servants and teachers.

However, many Labour MPs did not agree with the cuts, although they did agree with increasing income tax to 22.5 per cent. This was not enough to solve the problem. Bankers in America and Europe would not lend the British government any more money unless it took measures to spend less. The Liberals and Conservatives joined forces and voted together. They forced the government to set up a committee, known as the May Committee, to look at the problem. This committee recommended a cut in wages for all people employed by the government, as well as a 20 per cent reduction in unemployment benefit. Faced with a Labour Party which did not want to introduce these measures Ramsay MacDonald resigned.

On the very same day, 24 August 1931, MacDonald formed a coalition government with the Conservatives and Liberals. This government was known as the National Government.

The National Government

The majority of the Labour Party opposed MacDonald's decision to form a coalition government. Yet when an election was held in October 1931 those parties supporting the National Government won 554 seats, while the anti-MacDonald Labour Party won just 52.

The National Government carried out the recommendations made by the May report. All government employees had their wages cut by ten per cent, except for teachers, who had their wages cut by 15 per cent. The government also raised import duties to try and protect British industries and so prevent more unemployment. This is what Mosley had suggested. It didn't really work. It forced foreign industries to look for new countries to sell their goods in and so meant that British industries faced even more competition when they wanted to sell goods abroad. British exports fell. However, Britain did abandon the Gold Standard, which made British exports cheaper, especially when compared to goods from America and France. These two countries did not leave the Gold Standard until 1936.

Q

1 Look at source A.
a) What does the Labour cart represent?
b) What does the Labour horse represent?
c) Does the cartoonist support Labour's policies?

WAS THE GOVERNMENT ABLE TO DEAL WITH THE DEPRESSION?

By 1936 over 200 000 men had not had any work for over two years.

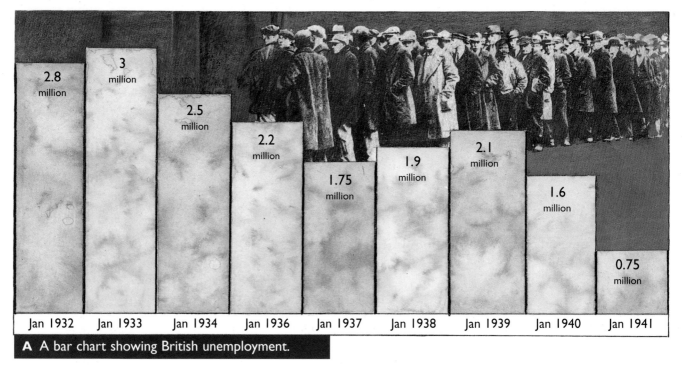

2.8 million	3 million	2.5 million	2.2 million	1.75 million	1.9 million	2.1 million	1.6 million	0.75 million
Jan 1932	Jan 1933	Jan 1934	Jan 1936	Jan 1937	Jan 1938	Jan 1939	Jan 1940	Jan 1941

A A bar chart showing British unemployment.

In his 1933 budget Neville Chamberlain, the Chancellor of the Exchequer and a Conservative, claimed that Britain had dealt with the Depression better than any other country. Was this true? Did the British government's actions control the level of unemployment? Or did the government's policies produce terrible suffering for the British people?

Government action

One further result of the May report was the introduction of the Means Test. This meant that if an unemployed person had some savings, they would get less benefit. Therefore if someone had been careful and saved a little money they would be paid less than someone who had spent all their money. The Means Test was hated by working people and many Labour-controlled local councils refused to use it. In 1934 the government took unemployment benefit out of the hands of local authorities and set up the Unemployment Assistance Board. If anything this was even more unpopular than the Means Test, since at first the rates it offered were even lower than before. However, in the same year Neville Chamberlain restored the wages of government employees to their old level, as well as raising unemployment benefit back to its previous figure.

B George Orwell, writing in 1937 (*The Road to Wigan Pier*).

When you see unemployment figures quoted at two millions, it is fatally easy to take this as meaning that two million people are out of work ... This is an enormous underestimate because ... the only people shown on unemployment figures are those drawing the dole [unemployment benefit] – that is, in general, heads of families.

Unlike America and Germany, Britain did not spend huge amounts of money to create jobs. The British government believed that a large government debt would produce far worse problems in the long term. Nevertheless, £2 million was spent on trying to attract industry to 'special areas', that is those areas with the worst unemployment. It made little difference. Money was loaned to the Cunard company to build the luxury liner the *Queen Mary*. The government also lent money so that inefficient coalmines and textile mills could be closed down. This helped those who were in work, since there was less competition for the goods they were producing. But it did nothing for those workers who were being made unemployed.

ARMAMENT FACTORY

HANDS WANTED

UNDERTAKER

HANDS WANTED

HANDS WANTED

Well done, sir. England is proud of you!

STATESMAN

ARMS RACKET

C A cartoon from the *Evening Standard*, 9 October 1933. This shows the effects of the government's policy of making more weapons. The statesman represents the government and the 'arms racket' represents the arms manufacturers.

The poor and the Depression

The most obvious effect of the Depression was unemployment. Yet even for those in work wages could be very low. In the 1930s health care was not free and so the poverty produced by the Depression led to a rise in ill-health, especially among children and the elderly. A survey carried out in Newcastle in the mid-1930s revealed that poor children were far more likely to suffer from ill health than rich children. Pneumonia was eight times more common and bronchitis ten times more common among the poor. A survey carried out in York in 1935–6 found that 43 per cent of the working class were living in poverty, and York didn't suffer from as much unemployment as many other northern cites.

Often poor people lived in terrible, overcrowded housing. In 1935 it was estimated that 12 per cent of the population lived more than two to a room. In other words a family of four were living in just two rooms. It was worse in many areas of London. In Finsbury 60 per cent of families lived in either one or two rooms. Liverpool had the worst slums in the country. In the St Anne's district of the city 20 000 people lived more than three to a room. The toilets for the houses were outside and the whole district was full of rats.

Hunger marches by the unemployed became common. The most famous of these occurred in 1936, when many of the people of Jarrow, a north-eastern shipbuilding town, marched to London to protest that the government was doing nothing to solve unemployment. At least two-thirds of the working population of Jarrow were unemployed. But the government refused to lend money to help to build a new steelworks in Jarrow.

Q

1 Look at source C.
   a) What is meant by the phrase 'hands wanted'?
   b) Only half the queue is going into the armaments factory. What is going to happen to the others?
   c) Does the cartoonist suggest that rearmament will create more jobs? Explain your answer.
   d) Does the cartoonist believe that rearmament will produce war and death? Explain your answer.
   e) Do you think that the cartoonist agrees with government policy on unemployment? Explain your answer.
2 Look at source A. What does it show about the level of unemployment in 1940 and 1941? Does this support the opinion of the cartoonist in source C?

Extended writing
Was the British government successful in dealing with unemployment in the 1930s? You should consider whether unemployment fell in the 1930s and what conditions were like for the unemployed.

WHO SUFFERED DURING THE DEPRESSION?

Not everywhere in Britain suffered equally from unemployment. It was in the old industrial areas that unemployment reached such terrible levels. Jarrow was a shipbuilding town which suffered when the Palmer's Shipyard, the only big company in the town, closed down in 1934. Merthyr Tydfil was a Welsh mining town. In 1926 there had been over one million miners in Britain. By 1934 there were less than 800 000. In contrast, many new consumer industries such as cars and electrical goods were booming, creating more jobs. If you had money you were better off. Prices fell in the 1930s. Well-off families had the money to buy these consumer goods.

SUPER 1933 HOMES

BARNEHURST PARK ESTATE BARNEHURST, KENT
Estate Office : Station Approach, Barnehurst, Kent.
Telephone : Bexleyheath 406.

9/6 WEEKLY
£395 FREEHOLD

NEW IDEAL HOMESTEADS LTD
BRITAIN'S BIGGEST BUILDERS

C An advertisement for new housing in south-east England. During the 1920s and 1930s treelined suburban developments had grown around the outside of London, offering family houses with large gardens.

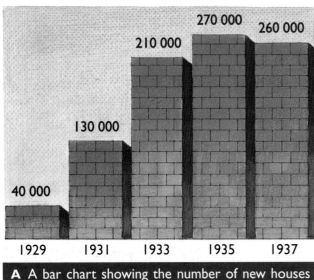

A A bar chart showing the number of new houses built by private companies betwen 1929 and 1937.

D Regional unemployment in Britain in 1934. This bar chart shows the percentage of workers unemployed in these towns in 1934.

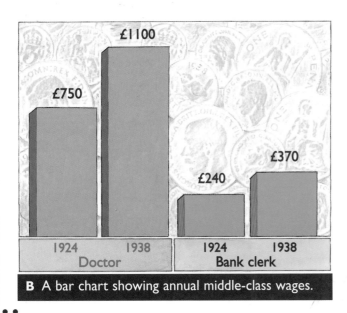

B A bar chart showing annual middle-class wages.

In 1936 7000 people were killed in road accidents, twice as many as in 1996.

THREE-SPEED TWO-SEATER
£100

FOUR-SPEED MODELS
from £105

E An advertisement for the Morris Minor. Car ownership increased dramatically in the 1930s. In 1929 the industry produced 180 000 cars. By 1938 production had almost doubled to 340 000.

F Dick Cunningham describes the middle-class house in which he was brought up in the 1930s.

When my father bought the house it had no electricity, just gas for lighting and cooking … and coal fires in every room. Before we moved in my father had electricity installed for lighting and plugs for lamps and electric fires … In the mid-thirties an electric heater was installed in a water tank … In the late thirties my mother had a small refrigerator, made by a reputable company, installed in the pantry. She discovered she was the first in her circle of friends to do so … We had two live-in servants, a cook and a housemaid, who shared the back bed-sitting room on the attic floor … the housemaids were aged fourteen to sixteen. As they usually had little or no experience they began on a monthly wage of [up to] 15 shillings [75 pence].

G Two historians give their interpretation (from *Britain in the Depression* by J Stevenson and C Cook, 1994).

It would be silly to suggest that the 1930s were not for many thousands of people a time of great hardship and personal suffering. But beside this picture of the unemployed must be put the other side of the case. There were never less than three-quarters of the population in work during the 1930s and for most of the period considerably more. Alongside the pictures of dole queues and hunger marches must also be placed those of another Britain, of new industries, prosperous suburbs and a rising standard of living.

H George Orwell, writing in 1937 (*The Road to Wigan Pier*).

To study unemployment and its effects you have got to go to the industrial areas. In the south unemployment exists but it is scattered … There are plenty of rural districts where a man out of work is almost unheard of.

1 What do sources C, E and F tell you about the 1930s?
2 What evidence can you find to back up the image created in these sources?
3 Look at source D. Which two towns suffer from the worst unemployment? Why was this?
4 The 1930s have been described as 'the hungry thirties'. Which sources support the view that the 1930s were a decade of poverty and suffering?
5 Source G refers to a decade where many people were well off and living standards rose. Which sources support this view?
6 The historians in source G describe Britain as a country of 'new industries, prosperous suburbs and a rising standard of living'. Source D shows that over 60 per cent of the workers in towns like Jarrow and Merthyr Tydfil were unemployed. How do you explain this difference in interpretation?

THE RISE AND FALL OF BRITISH FASCISM

Key Issue **Why did fascism fail to become popular in Britain?**

In June 1934 about 12 000 people turned up at London's Olympia. They had come to listen to a speech by Oswald Mosley, the leader of the British Union of Fascists (BUF). It was thought that at this time the BUF may have had as many as 50 000 members. It certainly had the support of the *Daily Mail*, which reported its activities in a favourable manner. Just over a year before, Hitler had become Chancellor of Germany. Over ten years earlier Mussolini had become the Prime Minister of Italy. Would Britain become the next fascist country? The BUF had money. Mussolini secretly gave the BUF £60 000 between 1933 and 1936. The favourable attitude of the *Daily Mail* meant that many middle-class people were willing to support Mosley. Perhaps he could solve the problems caused by the Depression.

As source A clearly shows the Olympia rally was not the springboard for fascist growth in Britain. It was the exact opposite. Why did support for the BUF collapse? Part of the reason was the Olympia rally itself. Mosley's speech was constantly interrupted by opponents of the fascists who were in the crowd. They were violently attacked and then thrown out by BUF stewards. Many middle-class people were frightened away by this violence. This impression was reinforced by the increased violence being used by Hitler in Germany.

Who was Oswald Mosley?

Like so many politicians in the 1930s Oswald Mosley had fought in the First World War. He believed that the terrible sufferings of the First World War were caused by the failure of the politicians to prevent war from breaking out. But he also felt that the First World War had brought the best out of the British people. If the sacrifices of the war were not to be wasted a new society must be built which encouraged the people to continue to work together for the benefit of everyone. The way to do this was to allow the government to continue to have the emergency powers it had gained during the war. Therefore in 1918 Mosley became a Conservative MP who supported the government of Lloyd George. He believed that Lloyd George would be the strong leader that Britain needed.

However, Mosley soon became disillusioned with the government because it returned to pre-war policies. In 1920 he left the Conservative Party and became an independent MP. Then in 1924 Mosley joined the Labour Party. He felt that socialism would organise society for the benefit of everyone. In 1929 he became a minister in the Labour government. Yet he was soon disillusioned by this government as well. He felt that it followed exactly the same policies as the Conservatives. In 1930 he resigned from the government.

In 1932 Mosley founded the BUF. They wore black shirts like Mussolini's fascists and they used a lightning symbol which looked like the Nazi swastika.

What did the fascists stand for?

The BUF always stressed a patriotic message. It would make Britain great again. The main problem facing Britain was the unemployment created by the Depression. Mosley promised to cure this with a programme of government spending. As in Germany, roads and public buildings would be built to create jobs. Britain and its empire would create a self-sufficient **economic bloc**. Unfortunately for the fascists the policies of the National Government gradually began to reduce unemployment. This meant that the middle classes were less likely to turn to fascism.

A Membership of the BUF.

50 000 — 1934
5000 — 1935
16 500 — 1938
22 500 — 1939

B Mosley addresses a fascist rally at the Empire Pool at Wembley.

The end of the BUF

After the collapse of the BUF membership in 1934 the message changed. Hatred of the Jews – anti-semitism – became the main message. The problems of working people were blamed on the Jews. This message found support in the East End of London. On 4 October 1936 Mosley organised a fascist march through the East End. About 3000 fascist supporters turned up, but they were faced by a crowd of 100 000 anti-fascists. The police banned the march and the fascists left under police protection. Over 100 people were injured as the anti-fascists clashed with the police. This became known as the Battle of Cable Street. The government reacted by passing the Public Order Act. This made it illegal for the blackshirts to wear their uniforms or to act as stewards at political meetings. It made it much more difficult for the BUF to create the sort of chaos which the SA had been able to cause in Germany in the years before Hitler came to power.

However, even in the East End the BUF received only limited support. When candidates stood in council elections in the East End in 1937 they got only 20 per cent of the vote.

In 1938 the BUF adopted yet another new policy – 'Stop the War'. With the danger of war in Europe Mosley suggested that Germany should be allowed to do what it wanted in eastern Europe.

The world's major powers should then negotiate a disarmament agreement. This message was much more popular than anti-semitism and BUF membership began to grow again. But war did break out and Mosley and over 700 other leading fascists were put in prison.

Q

1 Look at source B. How does the layout of the rally create the impression of a powerful leader?
2 How does the rally show the patriotism of the BUF?
3 Why do you think that Mussolini had to give money secretly to the BUF? How do you think people would have reacted if they knew that the BUF was being funded by Italian money?

Extended writing
What reasons can you find to explain why the BUF did not succeed in becoming a major political party in Britain? You should look at:
   a) the level of unemployment
   b) anti-semitism
   c) British relations with Germany
   d) The Public Order Act.

9

The Impact of the Second World War

How did the British people cope with the Blitz?

A Bomb damage. A bus has fallen into a bomb crater in Acton. The government did not allow this picture to be published at the time. Many pictures of bomb damage were censored.

In early 1940 Hitler launched his *Blitzkrieg* ('lightning war') on western Europe. One after another the countries of western Europe fell to the advancing Germans. Only Britain remained. But before the German army could successfully invade Britain, the Germans needed to destroy the RAF. In August and September 1940 the Battle of Britain was fought between the two airforces. Then on 7 September the German tactics changed. British cities would be bombed to destroy the resistance of the British people. The Blitz had begun. From 7 September to 2 November London was bombed every night. Then the Germans started to bomb other British cities as well. On 14 November the centre of Coventry was destroyed and 544 people were killed. Other cities such as Plymouth, Southampton and Liverpool soon suffered similar raids. For the rest of the winter the bombs rained down on British cities. But the Blitz was virtually over by the spring of 1941. The Germans needed to prepare for the invasion of Russia. Britain was no longer the number one target.

What were the effects of the Blitz?

Large numbers of civilians were killed during the Blitz. In 1940 over 23 000 civilians died in German bombing raids. In every week of September 1940 about 50 000 were made homeless. The damage to buildings was enormous.

The Blitz changed the lives of everyone who managed to survive. At night a blackout was enforced. In an attempt to confuse German bombers there were no streetlights. Cars were not allowed to use headlights. Blackout curtains were fitted to the windows of every house to stop light from leaking out. A city which did not show any light would be difficult for German bombers to hit. But the downside was that it became much more dangerous to drive a car. Deaths from road

B An Anderson shelter in operation. A family of five in a space just seven feet by five feet.

accidents more than doubled. 1500 people were killed in road accidents in December 1939, and the bombing hadn't even begun.

However, the Blitz was also meant to destroy Britain's industrial production. This it failed to do. Many new factories were moved away from the big cities. In the short term this cut production but once the Blitz was over the old and the new factories were combined to produce much more. Also the German planes were not really designed for the Blitz. Each raid would only drop about 100 tons of bombs on a city. Later in the war British planes would be able to drop 1800 tons of bombs a night on a single German city. Despite the terrible damage Coventry's factories were in operation just five days after 14 November.

People were encouraged to build their own air raid shelters in the garden. These were known as Anderson shelters, after the Home Secretary who ordered them to be built. The local council would deliver the corrugated iron. Then it was up to the family to dig the hole and build the shelter. In London people preferred to use the underground, although this was not official policy. London flats lacked gardens for shelters and the underground tunnels were far deeper. But they were not totally safe. During one raid a bomb hit Bank station and fell down the lift shaft. Apart from those killed by the blast many others were thrown onto the line and electrocuted.

C Londoners packed in an underground station during an air raid.

D Bernard Kops remembers running to the underground in an air raid.

After the terror of that night [7 September] people wanted to get underground. Thousands upon thousands pushed their way into Liverpool Street station, demanding to be let down to shelter. At first the authorities wouldn't agree and called out soldiers to bar the way. I stood there in the thick of the crowd, thinking there would be a panic and we would all be crushed … A great yell went up and the gates were opened … So I dashed with the crowd into the underground … No laughter, no humour. What sort of victory had we achieved? Every family for itself now.

E A young girl remembers what it was like to survive a nearby bomb blast.

Another bomb, nearer. Then, suddenly, the weirdest scratching sound just above the roofs – as if someone was scratching the sky with a fingernail. Then the most Godawful crash – it seemed only a couple of gardens away … I remember racing towards the house. The oddest feeling in the air all around, as if the whole air was falling apart, quite silently. And then suddenly I was on my face, just inside the kitchen door. There seemed to be waves buffeting me, one after another, just like bathing in a rough sea.

F Anne Valery remembers what it was like to find a home destroyed.

It was the small things that broke your heart. The sliced house exposing a nail holding a flannel; the fork protruding from a mountain of rubble; the burst pillow lying in the mud; and if one day you arrived home to find it gutted, it was a shattered pencil box that caused you to break down and cry.

Q

1 Why do you think that the government did not allow pictures such as source A to be published at the time they were taken?
2 What does source D tell you about how people reacted to the Blitz?
3 How effective was the Blitz? Explain your answer.

A COMMON AND UNITED DETERMINATION?

A A government poster warning everyone to carry gas masks. In fact the Germans never did attack with gas.

B Gas masks were carried by everyone. Do you think children really wore them to play? Why do you think that this photograph was taken?

C John Geer remembers what it was like to wear a gas mask when he was ten.

Although I could breathe in it, I felt as if I couldn't. It didn't seem possible that enough air was coming through the filter. The covering over my face … made me feel panicky.

On 27 April 1937 a new type of war was unleashed. German planes of the Condor legion bombed the Spanish city of Guernica. 800 civilians were killed. Civilians were now in the front line in a modern war. The British were determined not to be caught out by a repeat of the tactic. At the start of the war people of all ages were issued with gas masks. They were told to carry them at all times. In fact no gas attack was ever launched on Britain.

Evacuation

Evacuation began on 30 August 1939. Children who went to primary school were ordered out of the major cities. So were children under five years old, though they could take their mothers with them. The other children said goodbye to their families. They were sent to areas that the government thought would not be bombed. Altogether one and a half million children were moved by the government in the early days of the war. A further two million were moved privately. People sent them to relatives in the country.

D Children waiting to be evacuated. They have labels on them so they can be identified.

But no bombs came in the first months of the war. By January 1940 most of the children were back in the cities. Then came the Blitz. Once more children were parted from their families and sent to safety. This meant being sent to live with families who had never met them before. Many didn't want the children, but there was a war on, and the families were paid 7s 6d (37½ pence) a week. Although the government hoped that families and indeed schools would be kept together this was usually not possible. As sources E and F show, the experiences of the children could be very different.

Clarence [Caine's three-year-old brother] and I used to sleep together and poor Clarence used to wet the bed, 'cause he was a very nervous kid. She could never tell who'd done it so she used to bash the daylights out of both of us. So, of course, the more Clarence got hit the more he wet the bed. It was then we started to get locked in the cupboard. We weren't locked in the cupboard all the time, just when she used to go shopping … At the same time Clarence had a broken arm. This happened when we were coming out of the cupboard and the woman had hit him with a tennis racket.

F Eric Buchanan remembers his experience of leaving the city for the countryside.

It was marvellous. A smallholding outside the village. Again I was the only child … Being on my own, I used to wander around and explore the countryside. I remember on a summer's day, lying in a field and looking up at the blue sky and watching skylarks. And all around were yellow summer flowers. It was my first taste of the beauty of the countryside. I remember seeing a watermill where they made cider.

One result of evacuation was that it introduced many country people to city children. The children from the slums were often ill and underfed. It shocked country people, and helped to convince them that free health care for all was needed.

Were the British people united?

G Connie Brown remembers surviving a bomb.

We could not have an Anderson shelter because we were a corner house. About 9 pm a 500 lb bomb fell in the back garden and we were all buried under the debris until about 5.30 am next day … Eventually I was released and, to add insult to injury, the man assisting me said 'You will be all right now, son'. Not very flattering for a nineteen-year-old girl. We lost our home and our belongings. The coal got in for the winter was looted [stolen] along with some unbroken moveable objects and clothing.

H Charles Green remembers the communal air raid shelters in Rotherham.

A big old fashioned tea urn stood in one corner and, would you believe it, someone had brought in an old piano … everyone was having a real old sing-song. We were met at the entrance to the shelter by a lady holding pint mugs of hot cocoa and a pasty and everyone entering the shelter got the same treatment.

I Reginald Nash remembers when some bombs hit an ammunition train.

Eight huge explosions, one after the other, rocked the house … Rat-a-tat-tat on the front door. 'I'm sorry sir but you and your family may have to evacuate these premises as there is an ammunition train on fire across the fields' … Several incendiaries [fire bombs] had caught the first two trucks of a train. Two rail-waymen, George Keen and George Leech, together with five unknown soldiers, managed to uncouple the untouched trucks and get them to safety. It was said at the time that if they hadn't acted as they did … the best part of the village would have been blown away.

J Robert Runcie, the former Archbishop of Canterbury, remembers the war.

Ordinary men and women endured the Blitz, and by faith and courage finally won through … Some stayed in their homes, making use of basements and cellars. Some used shelters, cold and wet as they often were … But throughout the land was a common and united determination.

Q

1 What do you think Archbishop Runcie meant by 'a common and united determination'?
2 Look back over the last four pages. Which sources back up Runcie's interpretation of the Blitz?
3 Which sources do not back up his interpretation?
4 Do you believe that the British people all worked together to survive the Blitz?

A NEW NATIONAL GOVERNMENT

In what ways did the role of the government change in the Second World War?

The lessons of the First World War had been learnt. The first time round the war had been half over before the government had taken control of large areas of public life. This time the change was almost immediate. Just like in the First World War it came with a change of prime minister. In May 1940 Churchill replaced Chamberlain. His National Government was rather different to Lloyd George's. As well as politicians from the three main parties, it also included people other than politicians. The newspaper owner Lord Beaverbrook was put in charge of aircraft production. This was a vital job as the Battle of Britain and then the Blitz got underway. Lord Woolton, who had been in charge of John Lewis stores in Manchester, was made the Minister of Food. The trade unionist, Ernest Bevin, became the Minister of Labour.

Industry

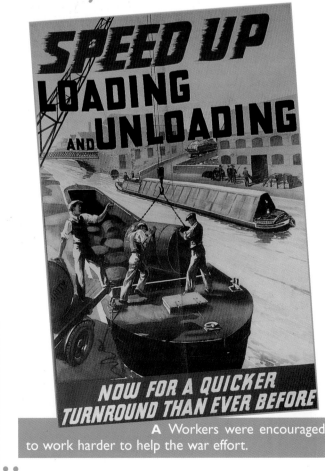

A Workers were encouraged to work harder to help the war effort.

As in the First World War the government took control of those industries which were vital to the war effort. The only exception was the mines, which were left in the hands of the private owners. The Ministry of Labour was given the power to move workers from one industry to another. They could, therefore, order men to become miners to increase production. This is what actually happened in 1943. Such men became known as the 'Bevin Boys', after the Minister of Labour who organised the scheme.

Bevin also introduced other changes to boost production. He agreed to ban strikes and to remove the limits on the number of hours that could be worked. During the Battle of Britain workers in factories making planes had to work 112 hours a week. In return workers were guaranteed a minimum wage. Men working in the aircraft factories could earn as much as £20 a week, at a time when the average wage was just £6.50. However, strikes still did take place. There were a number of strikes by miners. They were unhappy that women in aircraft factories could earn more than they did. Miners demanded a wage of £6 a week.

1938	1 334 000
1939	1 356 000
1940	940 000
1941	1 079 000
1942	1 527 000
1943	1 808 000
1944	3 714 000
1945	2 835 000

B Days lost through strikes.

At first Lord Beaverbrook was put in charge of aircraft production. Aircraft were desperately needed to prevent the German invasion. 'Saucepans for Spitfires' was the slogan for the campaign to encourage people to give up their aluminium pans so that more planes could be built. It helped people to feel that they were taking part in the war effort. However, it did little to build planes. The aluminium was rarely of good enough quality. Britain had enough aluminium. The problem was turning it into planes. This was overcome by removing the limits on working hours. By the end of the Battle of Britain the RAF had more planes than it had started with, despite the fact that 185 planes had been shot down by the Germans.

C 'Saucepans for Spitfires.' A Chelsea Pensioner, a veteran of earlier wars, gives an aluminium pot.

Beaverbrook later became Minister for Supply. This put him in control of all production for the war. By 1942 the army had enough rifles for the next ten years and enough troop carrying vehicles for another four years. The Ministry of Supply also controlled the railways. They were still organised as four independent systems, as they had been since the end of the First World War. Unfortunately there were not enough links between the systems. This meant loaded wagons got stuck where they weren't needed.

Conscription

Britain's army was not a volunteer army in the Second World War. Conscription began in the summer of 1939, before the war had even started. The result was a dramatic increase in the size of the armed forces, as source D shows. All men between the ages of 18 and 41 could be called up. In 1941 conscription was extended to women as well.

	Army	Navy	Air Force
1939	241 000	129 000	113 000
1940	1 656 000	276 000	291 000
1945	2 931 000	789 000	963 000

D The British armed forces during the Second World War.

Dad's Army

However, there was a volunteer army on the home front in the Second World War. It was the Home Guard. There was a great fear of a German invasion. Therefore all men who had not been called up were asked to volunteer for this army, whose job was to defend Britain from the invading German army. It consisted of men who were in essential industries, such as train drivers and miners, as well as those who were too old to be conscripted. By June 1940 five million men had joined up, though there were not nearly enough equipment and uniforms for them all. Because of the age of so many of its members the Home Guard was known as 'Dad's Army'.

E Dad's Army in action. This is grenade throwing practice.

Q

1 Did the 'Saucepans for Spitfires' campaign help to produce more planes for the RAF? Explain your answer.
2 Do you think that the campaign did any good at all?

Extended writing
Look back to Chapter 4. In what ways was government policy in the First World War similar to government policy in the Second World War, and in what ways were they different?
   You should refer to the following areas in your answer:
   a) rationing
   b) conscription
   c) strikes
   d) unions
   e) members of the government.

MORE GOVERNMENT – MORE FOOD?

In one important respect the Second World War was very like the First World War. Britain's food supplies were threatened by German U-boats. In April 1941 700 000 tons of shipping were sunk by U-boats.

Rationing

Rationing was introduced in January 1940. This time the British government did not wait until the war was almost over before controlling food supplies. Rationing had two aims.

1 Everyone had to 'tighten their belts'. Less food had to be eaten since the U-boat attacks meant that there wasn't as much food available.
2 Food supplies would be distributed equally. Everyone received exactly the same. This meant that poor people got exactly the same food as the rich. Unlike in the 1930s poor people at last had enough to eat. Children were given the same amount as an adult, except that they got an extra half pint of milk a day. Babies and young children got cod liver oil and rose hip syrup as well. This produced a very healthy generation of young children.

A ration book contained vouchers for various types of food. Everything was rationed except seasonal fruit and vegetables. The ration book meant that everyone ate a very healthy diet. Meat was in very short supply. Everyone hoped the butcher would give them some extra.

A Rationing made the butcher a very important person. Anne Valery remembers the role of the butcher in *Talking about the War.*

> Standing like some high priest, knife poised in the sceptre position behind his marble altar, the butcher was not only wooed with sweet words, but tickets to this and that and much under the counter barter.

Lord Woolton

Food rationing was run by the Ministry of Food. This was headed by Lord Woolton, a successful businessman. He was responsible for a number of schemes to encourage people to make the best use of the food available. 'Food facts' were printed in newspapers and magazines. They explained why types of food were in short supply. They also gave recipes for those foods which were available. Since potatoes were always available they formed the basis

B Dr Carrot. People were encouraged to use the food which was available.

C A government poster. People were encouraged to grow their own food.

of many of the recipes – including sandwiches, puddings and cakes! 'Food flashes' also appeared after the news on radio. Two cartoon characters, Dr Carrot and Potato Pete were created. 'Eat us', they cried. Other recipes showed people how to make food go further. Flour could be used so that one egg could make six omelettes. Clothing was rationed as well.

Woolton also encouraged people to 'Dig for Victory'. This meant growing more food themselves. Roadside verges and golf courses were dug up and planted with vegetables. Gardening clubs were formed so that tools could be shared. Even children took part.

How efficiently did the government run the British economy?

During the war the government was able to control a great many aspects of the life of the country. But did it do so efficiently?

The historian Corelli Barnett points out that British industrial production was much less efficient than other countries. It took three times as long to build a Spitfire as it did to build a

'We could do with thousands more like you..'

JOIN THE WOMEN'S LAND ARMY

D
As in the First World War women were encouraged to join the Women's Land Army. As in the First World War it was not popular. Work on farms could be very tough and very dirty.

E A comparison of British and German aircraft production during the Second World War. Remember that Britain had a smaller population than Germany.

Year	Britain	Germany
1939	7 900	8 300
1940	15 000	10 200
1941	20 500	11 800
1942	23 700	15 400
1943	26 300	24 800
1944	26 500	39 800

F Correlli Barnett on Britain's performance during the war (adapted from *Britain 1918–51*, edited by P Catterall, 1994).

The secret files of the Cabinet make it clear, that 'the British disease' as we now recognise it, was widespread in war ... British industry was only four-fifths as efficient as German industry and less than half as efficient as American.

German Messerschmidt ME 109. British industry depended on the American 'lend lease' agreement. From late 1940 onwards America provided Britain with equipment. This meant that Britain would have to pay for it later. Britain needed automatic lathes to help manufacture weapons. In 1942 Britain was forced to import almost three times as many lathes from America as British factories were able to make for themselves. Barnett also points out that British factories were hit by what was later called the 'British disease' – strikes. In the first three months of 1944 two million tons of coal were lost through strikes. In the dockyards there were strikes about dilution (see page 16). Skilled workers protected their jobs. The Amalgamated Engineers Union refused to let rail workers work in the docks. A report on the docks in 1942 complained that workers always started work 15 minutes late and ended 15 minutes early.

In 1943 children collected half a million tons of rose hips, enough for syrup for every baby in England.

G A different view of the government's performance, from a British historian, H L Peacock, in *A History of Modern Britain* (1982).

The great increase in the power of the Central Government over many aspects of the life of the individual was very significant ... these controls were both very necessary and highly effective.

Q

1 Read source F. What does Barnett mean by the 'British disease'?
2 Look at source C on page 56. Does this back up Barnett's opinion about the 'British disease'?
3 Look at pages 17 and 54. Were strikes more of a problem in the First or the Second World War?
4 Does Barnett believe that the British government ran the economy efficiently? Explain your answer.
5 What impression is given by source G?
6 Barnett, in source F, has claimed that British industry was not as efficient as it should have been. Using your own knowledge and the sources in this chapter, explain whether you agree or disagree with this interpretation.

10

The New Jerusalem?

Why was a welfare state introduced after the Second World War? How successful was it?

Between 1944 and 1951 Britain set up a welfare state. The government attempted to provide all the services needed to keep people healthy and to get rid of poverty. Everyone was to have a right to a minimum standard of living. The people of Britain had been promised a land fit for heroes after the First World War but it had never happened. The combined effect of the 1930s and the Second World War meant that people were determined to create a better Britain this time around.

The Thirties

The Liberal reforms of 1906–11 could not cope with the poverty and unemployment produced by the Depression (see pages 42–47). People's health suffered from the poverty. It cost money to see a doctor and still more if you needed a prescription. In the 1930s many people couldn't afford to go to the doctor.

B David Taylor remembers his young days in the slums of Manchester (quoted in *The Nineties* by Wood and Thompson, 1993).

> Scarlet fever and diphtheria were common. There was always the yellow van coming down from Monsal Fever Hospital carting them away. I think it was the hygiene conditions which caused such a lot of diphtheria and the other illnesses. And the death rate was very, very high with children.
>
> It was a common saying that 'you're never a mother until you've lost one.' I should think nearly every woman in those days lost one. They just had the ordinary midwife come to them, and she used to do the job, and if it wasn't done proper the mother died or the child died.

The Second World War

German bombing caused enormous numbers of casualties. The government had no choice – it simply had to provide free hospital care for everyone. People were having their houses destroyed. They could hardly be expected to pay for their hospital treatment. Therefore a national

A The remains of South Hallsville school in London. On 10 September 1940 around 400 people were killed when the school was hit by a bomb. Most of the dead were women and children waiting to be evacuated.

C A *Daily Herald* cartoon from 2 December 1942. The *Daily Herald* was a paper which traditionally supported the Labour Party.

TACKLING THE FIRST GIANT

"WANT is only one of the five giants on the road of reconstruction" — The Beveridge Report.

system of free hospital care, under the control of the government, came into existence during the war. If Britain could provide free care during the crisis of a war then why not also in peacetime?

> The term 'a New Jerusalem' referred to a time when workers would not be forced to live and work in terrible conditions. Everyone, and not just the rich, would get good housing and free health care.

William Beveridge – slayer of giants

During the war the government asked for a number of reports to draw up plans for rebuilding Britain after the war. The most important of the reports was drawn up by William Beveridge.

Beveridge suggested that there were five 'giants' which would have to be slain before Britain could create a better society. These giants were: 'Want' – lack of food and the basics for life; 'Disease' – avoidable illness; 'Idleness' – unemployment; 'Ignorance' – lack of education for all; 'Squalor' – poverty. In order to defeat these 'giants' Beveridge proposed setting up a welfare system which was open to everyone, regardless of their wealth. There would be no return to the hated Means Test. The system would also establish a minimum standard of living. No matter how poor people were the system would ensure that they had a reasonable standard of living. To achieve this Beveridge made the following proposals.

1 An insurance scheme to cover people against unemployment, sickness and old age. Everyone would pay the same contribution and everyone would receive the same benefits.
2 The unemployed would receive their benefits for as long as they were unemployed.
3 Every family would receive an allowance for every child. Children who had been part of large, poor families had often suffered terribly from ill-health.
4 A free national health service for everyone. Poor people would be able to go to the doctor and get good medical attention.

The state would look after its citizens 'from the cradle to the grave'. The Beveridge report summed up the hopes of so many British people. Within a year it had sold over half a million copies.

Q

1 Which giant does source D show as the first one to be dealt with?
2 Look at source D. What impression is it giving of Beveridge? How does it do this?
3 Show how the welfare state was supposed to slay three of Beveridge's five giants.
4 Which giant do you believe the government should slay first? Explain your answer.

LABOUR'S WELFARE STATE

AND NOW – WIN THE PEACE

VOTE LABOUR

A A Labour poster from 1945. Labour were promising the land fit for heroes which had not been built after the First World War.

YOUR **BRITAIN**

disease

FIGHT FOR IT NOW

B This poster was issued by the National Government in 1944. Yet it was quickly withdrawn. It promised an end to disease. Churchill feared that the government was making promises which it might not be able to deliver.

The National Government had drawn up a number of plans to rebuild Britain before the end of the war. The Education Act had been introduced in 1944. This gave free secondary education to everyone between the ages of 11 and 15 for the first time ever. The National Government also introduced the Family Allowance Act in June 1945. Every family would receive five shillings (25 pence) a week for every child after the first.

However, in July 1945 Labour won the general election with a huge majority. Labour won 393 seats while the Conservatives won just 197. The voters believed that the Labour Party was more likely than the Conservatives to carry out the promises made by the National Government during the war. Although the Beveridge report was the work of the National Government, the voters believed that Labour was more committed to Beveridge's proposals. The reforms fitted in well with socialist beliefs. A free health service would be available for all regardless of wealth. It would be paid for by taxation. The richer you were the more you would contribute.

The Labour reforms

The National Insurance Act 1946
Everyone who worked was also able to claim benefit when they were unable to work. If you were ill, unemployed, pregnant or too old you received the benefit. The scheme was financed by contributions from both workers and employers. All workers paid the same contributions regardless of how much they earned since they all received the same benefit. However, although sickness benefit could be claimed for an unlimited length of time, unemployment benefit could only be claimed for six months. None of the benefits were means tested, but they were set at a level which was lower than that received by people in low paid jobs.

The National Health Service Act 1946
This set up a national health service which came into being in 1948. Free health care was provided for all. Unlike the Liberal reforms of 1906–11 hospital treatment, medicine, dental care and opticians would now all be free, as well as visits to the doctor. Also, everyone was covered, not just the person in work.

The National Assistance Act 1948
In order to slay the giant 'want' everyone needed to be guaranteed a minimum income. This Act made sure that everyone had some money. It gave benefits to those who failed to qualify under the National Insurance scheme because they had not

made any contributions. However, a form of means test was introduced for these benefits. The Act ordered local councils to provide housing for old and handicapped people. Temporary housing also had to be provided for the homeless.

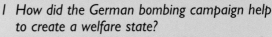

1 How did the German bombing campaign help to create a welfare state?

2 An opinion poll revealed that 86 per cent of British people thought that Beveridge's recommendations should be made law. Why do you think that his proposals were so popular with so many people?

3 Did the Labour and National governments carry out all of Beveridge's proposals?
   a) Fill in the table below by putting a tick or a cross in the boxes to confirm whether or not Beveridge's proposals were fully carried out.
   b) For each box with a cross explain the way in which Beveridge's proposals were not fully carried out.

Beveridge report	The National Government	Labour 1945–51
A single system to cover everyone		
Everyone has to make the same financial contribution		
All benefits to be paid without time limit		
Family allowance for each child		
Free health care for all		

Extended writing
'The welfare state which was set up by the Labour Party after the war did not go far enough in helping Britain's poor.' Using the sources on pages 59–60 and your own knowledge, explain whether you agree or disagree with this interpretation.

NATIONALISATION

Between 1945 and 1950 the Labour government created a welfare state which covered everyone. This was not the end of their reforms. They also took over the main industries of the country. This was called nationalisation. It was not new to Britain. During the First World War the railways and the mines had been taken over by the government. In 1926 the Central Electricity Generating Board had been created as a government-controlled company to produce electricity. These nationalisations had occurred either to make sure that the industries served the needs of the country in war, or to ensure that the economy functioned efficiently.

In 1945 Labour had another motive. As a socialist party they believed that privately run industry could lead to the needs of the workers being ignored. This would only stop if the government owned the factories, mines and transport system. This was set out in Clause Four of the constitution of the Labour Party. No longer would high profits for the owners be the main concern. Safer working conditions and less unemployment would be more important.

In 1947 the coal industry was nationalised and this was followed in 1948 by the nationalisation of the railways. Both needed huge amounts of money to replace their old equipment and only the government could afford this. In 1948 the supply of electricity and gas was also nationalised.

Were the Labour reforms a success?

In its first year of operation 95 per cent of the population joined the National Health Service (NHS). As sources A and B suggest it did a great deal of good for a great many people. However, the historian Correlli Barnett has suggested that, despite its undoubted popularity, the NHS has not been a success. The Liberals, who had introduced social reforms at the beginning of the century, had wanted to produce fitter workers so that British industry could compete with foreign industry. Barnett says that this is how the NHS should be judged. At the end of the war Britain spent huge amounts of money on the NHS. It cost £400 million in its first year. Barnett believes that this money should have been spent on updating British industry, as happened in Germany. Only when the modernised industry had created wealth should money have been spent on a health service. Instead an increasingly uncompetitive British industry was having to fund an increasingly expensive health service.

A Philip Sauvain, a historian, writing in 1987 in his book *British Economic and Social History*.

In its initial stages the NHS was the envy of the world. The improvements in medical care were clear for all to see, most noticeably in the maternity wards, where infant deaths fell sharply. Older people benefited enormously from better fitting teeth, the use of good quality spectacles and effective hearing aids.

B Death of children under the age of one year.

| 1933 | 64 deaths per 1000 children |
| 1956 | 25 deaths per 1000 children |

C A *Daily Mirror* cartoon from May 1946.

D Nye Bevan, speaking at the Labour Party conference of 1945. Bevan was the Health Minister who set up the National Health Service.

We are the memories of the bitter years. We are the voice of the British people ... We have been the dreamers, we have been the sufferers, we are the builders.

E Correlli Barnett, writing in 1995 (adapted from *The Lost Victory*).

The dreamers of New Jerusalem ignored the real life problem of paying for its creation out of what was a bankrupt and backward industrial economy.

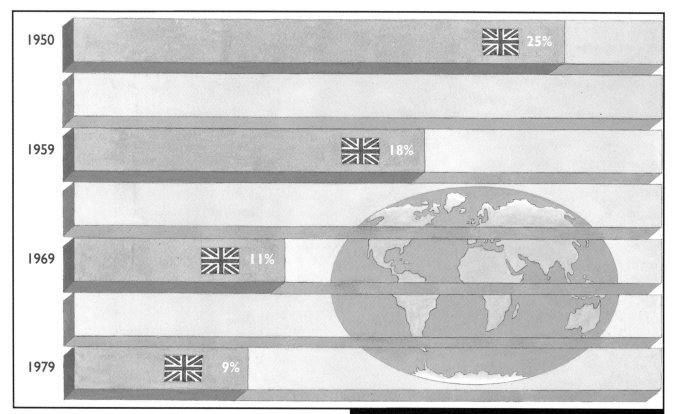

1950		25%
1959		18%
1969		11%
1979		9%

G British share of world trade in manufactured goods.

H The cost of the welfare state – government spending on welfare.

1935	£274 000 000
1955	£1 324 000 000

Into the twenty-first century

Better health care for everyone has enabled people to live longer and has helped the size of the British population to grow. This means that increasing numbers of people in Britain now require health care, and, as many modern treatments are very expensive, the overall cost of health care has risen dramatically. Another consequence of a larger and older population is that more people require pensions for longer periods of time. Again, this costs more money. Can Britain still afford a welfare state which provides pensions and free health care for everyone? Should people pay for private health care and private pensions? Will the welfare state survive the twenty-first century? These are all questions which will have to be addressed by governments who come and go.

F Nye Bevan, speaking in 1948.

The rush for spectacles, as for dental treatment, has exceeded all expectations. Part of what has happened has been a natural first flush of success of the new scheme, with the feeling that everything is free now and it does not matter what is charged to the government.

Q

1 Why do you think that 95 per cent of the British people joined the NHS in its first year?
2 Why was the cost of the welfare state so high?
3 Which sources support the view that Labour was right to introduce its reforms?
4 Which sources support Barnett's view that the country could not afford to spend so much on health?

Extended writing
Correlli Barnett, in source E, has suggested that the British government should have invested more money in modernising British industry rather than creating a national health service after the war. Using the sources and your own knowledge, explain whether or not you agree with this interpretation.

Glossary

censored – the government checked all information before it was published. Nothing could be published if it was felt to be a danger to national security

coalition – a government formed by two or more different parties

conscription – the compulsory recruitment of men, and sometimes women, into the armed forces

dilution – semi-skilled and unskilled workers were allowed to do jobs which had previously only been carried out by skilled workers. Naturally skilled workers resented dilution

direct action – to try and influence the government and public opinion by strikes or protests which might break the law

economic bloc – a group of countries which trade together

empire – a group of colonies under the rule of another country

free trade – there are no import and export duties when goods are sold to foreign countries. This means that the goods are cheaper and so more are sold

friendly societies – for a small weekly payment friendly societies provided workers with money when they were ill

Industrial Revolution – the rapid development of British industry by use of machines in the early nineteenth century

nationalised industry – an industry which has been converted from private to government ownership

propaganda – persuading people to believe in certain ideas and behave in a certain way; sometimes involves the telling of lies

provenance – where a source comes from. Who wrote it? When? Who was intended to read it? What role did the writer have?

revolution – the violent overthrow of a government in order to put another government in power

socialism – a system of government which supports democracy and a greater government involvement in economy and society

Trades Union Congress (TUC) – an official body which represents the trade unions in Britain

war of attrition – a war where both parties were trying to win by wearing down the other army, inflicting such terrible casualties that the enemy would give in

Index